STALKING
TROPHY
BROWN TROUT

A Fly-Fisher's Guide to Catching the Biggest Trout of Your Life

John Holt

Photographs by Ginny Holt

LYONS PRESS

Guilford, Connecticut

An imprint of Globe Pequot Press

To buy books in quantity for corporate use
or incentives, call **(800) 962-0973**
or e-mail **premiums@GlobePequot.com**.

Lyons Press is an imprint of Globe Pequot Press.

Interior photos by Ginny Holt.

Text design: Sue Murray
Project editor: Heather Santiago
Layout artist: Sue Murray

Library of Congress Cataloging-in-Publication Data is available on file.

ISBN 978-0-7627-7389-3

Printed in the United States of America
10 9 8 7 6 5 4 3 2 1

The book is dedicated to the memory of Betty Welles,

who showed me the possibilities for magic

in both fly fishing and life.

The author and photographer will donate 25 percent of the royalties earned from this book to the Alliance for the Wild Rockies (www.wildrockiesalliance.org).

Contents

Acknowledgments

I wish to acknowledge my editor, Allen Jones, who first encouraged the idea that became this book. We've worked together over many years on a number of projects and become friends in the process. The following were generous with their advice, tips, and observations: David Decker, Forrest Glover, Jake Howe, Joe Kipp, Dan Lahren, Powell Swanser, and John Talia. When I needed specific equipment and advice, these people came through in the clutch: Nate Dablock at Cortland, Matt Crawford of Simms, Steve Krewson at Hardy, the crew at Tropical Sea, and Rich Paini at TroutHunter. They all pitched in to make researching and photographing this book easier and more productive. As always, Ginny's photographs are what makes any book she and I do together special. She sees the world through eyes that help me experience good country as a child once again.

Introduction

He is thus like a boy going off for the long vacation. It is thus with all of us. Once an angler, always a fisherman. If we cannot have the best, we will take the least, and fish for minnows if nothing better is to be had.

—Theodore Gordon, 1912

Fly fishing is a passion that has evolved into a way of life over the past fifty years. At first this was something that happened more or less by itself, but as time passed the passion also became a benign obsession fueled by my desire to spend as much time in country where trout live. Now I live in Livingston, Montana, and if you know anything about the area, then you know that it has no shortage of fishing, from the Yellowstone River to the Paradise Valley spring creeks to nearby rivers, including the Gallatin, Boulder, and Madison.

My grandmother was a fly fisher from way back in the late 1920s. She nurtured my interest with stories of Alaska, Wyoming, and Norway, to name a few, along with loaning me books on the subject. By the time I moved to Montana more than forty years ago, I exclusively fly fished (though I have been backsliding into bait fishing for catfish on the Little Powder—treble hooks, chicken livers, big sinkers, and cats to 15 pounds). I was not any good at the art, but I was fortunate to be surrounded by superb trout waters and even more blessed to meet talented and knowledgeable individuals like Glenn West, who started the original Grizzly Hackle fly shop way back when Missoula was a small town of 15,000. It was at this small shop that I made the acquaintance and quickly the friendship of the late Harmon Henkin. Glenn and Harmon pointed me in directions that led to a deeper appreciation of fly

Montana resident John Talia displays a brown trout he took during the fall.

fishing and in turn made me a more accomplished angler. Since then I've fished with wonderful people—Bob Jones, Tom Rosenbauer, Tim Tollett, Tim Mosolf, John Talia, Gary LaFontaine, and a bunch of others, all superb fishermen and human beings.

As the years passed I got better at catching brown trout, big ones. I couldn't help myself, given all the generous advice from my friends and the transitional function of experience translating, in a largely subconscious way, to physical actions on the river, methods that are close to automatic, as natural to me as walking. Before beginning to write this book, I spent a lot of time examining what it is I do that now leads to regularly catching big browns, along with other trout species, where ten years ago this was not the case (with the exception of fishing rivers like the Jefferson, upper Clark Fork, and Beaverhead when they were hot, something that holds true for most of us). I realized that I'll never be considered an artful caster, although I'm good at putting a fly where I want it to go at distances up to 60 feet, even when it's breezy. After that it's often a crapshoot. But as Lefty Kreh said, "Most fishermen use the double haul to throw their casting mistakes further."

In my way I put the fly where I want it well over 90 percent of the time. When coupled with being able to read water almost at a glance, I'm most often successful with casts of 40 feet and usually less. I know what types of retrieves and floats work well for large fish. And I have around two dozen patterns that I rely on to take fish—eight of which I use most of the time: Joe's Hopper, Woolly Bugger, Partridge and Orange Soft Hackle, Hare's Ear Nymph, Elk Hair Caddis, Yellow Humpy, Biggs' Special, and LaFontaine's Emergent Sparkle Pupa. If they don't produce, I'm doing something wrong, like fishing too fast or sloppily, both circumstances now rarities only because I've done this so many times over the decades while making mental and written notes on what has worked and what hasn't. All of the patterns I use are described in the appropriate chapters, including the tying recipes.

A big fish to one person may be considered less so by another. I don't advocate fishing solely with the intent of catching trophy trout or large numbers of fish; that's not how I see fly fishing. Getting out in good country, connecting with the natural world, making friends, and, of course, fishing and catching fish are all part of the experience. What I always take from a day fishing is a sense of balance and peace with the world.

A trophy brown can be a number of things. It is to some extent a matter of perspective. On the Yellowstone as it flows through Livingston, where I live, a fish over 5 pounds qualifies as a trophy. On the upper stretches of a tributary I fish often, a little stream where browns average 13 to 14 inches, a 2-pound trout is a serious fish. For someone who's never caught a brown larger than 20 inches (a nice fish anywhere, by the way), that first 25-inch brown trout is a moment to be cherished. So, as I said, "trophy" is in the eye of the beholder.

I remember my first brown of 5 pounds. It was taken on a large hopper pattern along a deep run above Turah on the Clark Fork River east of Missoula. I see it as though it happened this morning: the bug bouncing down the dark aquamarine river, and then the enormous bronze and white flash as the trout engulfed the fly. The fight was vigorous but never in doubt, given a stout tippet and plenty of open water on my side. I held the brown in the air for much longer than I do now, then revived and released it. I thought over and over to myself in the following days, "A 5-pound fish. I really can catch them that big." That moment on the Clark Fork changed my life—not just my fly-fishing life, my entire life. Almost all of what I've done since that day has revolved around having the freedom to go fishing whenever I want to, and to spending lots of time learning how to take big fish: browns, rainbows, bull trout, westslope cutthroats, smallmouth bass, northerns—all of them.

The largest brown trout I ever caught was just short of 30 inches and over 11 pounds, pulled from a small tributary of the Clark

Brown trout come in all sizes, and from some of the most unexpected types of water. This one was taken from a creek barely 6 feet wide.

Fork below Missoula, not far from the Idaho border. This was more than twenty years ago. Joe Huston, at the time a fisheries biologist for the Montana Department of Fish, Wildlife & Parks, had told me about several small, stream-specific spawning runs of enormous browns in the area. And by small runs Joe meant 100 to 350 fish in each stream. I've also caught migrating browns over 10 pounds in the streams of northern Wisconsin that empty into both Lake Superior and Lake Michigan. This was back in the late seventies when I worked briefly for a daily newspaper in southern Wisconsin. Not many fly fishers knew about these magnificent fish back then, so I had the water all to myself. One of the highlights was running into Robert Traver (aka John Voelker) in a tavern, where we shared more than a few cocktails. A great man with many fine thoughts on both angling and life.

The techniques described in this book will catch the larger browns in a given stretch of water. But even with all I've been shown and have learned over the years, I realize that I rarely come close to catching the largest brown in a river. This point was brought home a few years ago when a fisheries biologist told me that the largest trout they'd surveyed in the central Montana river where I was then fishing was over 17 pounds. The heaviest I'd taken that day was 8 pounds, while a friend had turned one that had been more like a dozen pounds. But far from finding the news discouraging, knowing that there were even larger browns in the water gave us added energy.

I also remember a fine day on Big Spring Creek when I took a good number of rainbows and browns. These were stocky fish, weighing 3 to 4 pounds. I thought I was quite the guy until I came up to a hole formed by water tumbling over a tree trunk embedded in the streambed. Looking down through 6 feet of water, I spotted a brown that had last seen 12 pounds some years ago. The fish was enormous. Nothing I sank down to it had any effect, either in a take or in spooking the leviathan. I've since learned that some huge trout

Years ago I would have passed over water like this, but some patient observation
revealed this lightly dappled stretch to be big trout country.

are virtually unattainable, much like world peace, a Cubs World Series appearance, or total serenity.

The majority of the waters mentioned here are in the West. I use them as examples because I know them better than rivers found in other parts of the country. This doesn't mean that methods and patterns discussed in the book will only work in the Rockies. What works where I fish will also be successful where you fish.

Tailwaters each have their own special set of circumstances, so they will be discussed in general terms. I will also discuss some river techniques that can be applied to stillwater fishing as well. I've found that what works in rivers will frequently work for still water, while the reverse is not often true.

The most important attribute of any fly fisher is the ability to recognize and analyze his experiences. As G. E. M. Skues said in *Itchen Memories:* "Many writers on angling urge their readers to observe. The trouble is that most of us observe without learning anything from it."

I was a poster child for this up until twenty years ago, and I can still fit the mold at times if I'm too eager or aggressive. If I make myself an obvious outsider, an anomaly in an environment of wild rhythms, I'll catch few if any fish, let alone large ones. I've learned to recognize this fast-passed futility, and can now catch myself, stop, breathe deeply, and enjoy my surroundings—mountains, clear water bubbling over a copper-colored streambed, blue sky, gentle breeze. Learning to slip into the natural flow of things is analogous to understanding what weight and type of line work best with a given rod. What fits is what works. Forcing things is futile.

This book is about what I've learned from more than fifty-five years of fishing, beginning back when I was three on Rice Lake, Wisconsin, fishing for sunfish with worms and a bobber. I expect that some readers will disagree with what I have to say. Take what appeals to you and reject or disprove the rest to your satisfaction. I must admit that the cant of fly fishing's "purists" used to annoy me. No longer. To each his own. None of what follows is dogma, nor do I consider these words to be angling gospel. They are merely the observations and attendant thoughts of someone who loves everything about hunting big brown trout—the good country, the weather, the waters, and the trout themselves.

CHAPTER 1

The Elusive, Predatory Nature of Browns

I frankly don't make much of a living, but I make a hell of a life.

—Jack Gartside

Browns have incredible personalities. A stupid rainbow always looks at the fly in his jaw as you remove it, where a brown looks you right in the eye . . . I have had them snap at the bill of my hat in the process of taking a photo, or even worse, when my friend David Decker (of the Complete Fly Fisher) was guiding a lady client who finally landed a 20-plus incher—she was so happy she decided to try to kiss the fish in the process of taking the photo— unfortunately she required stitches for her lip after the fish latched down on it—blood everywhere . . .

—John Talia

Why are browns so difficult to catch, and why is hunting this voracious predator so rewarding and exciting? How are browns different from other trout? The classic crouching, quiet approach with lengthy leaders, tiny tippets, and long casts is not usually needed for browns. Big patterns, short stout leaders, and loud, splashy casts tight to the bank or even onto the bank often work better. There are times when an angler needs to attract the attention of big fish that prefer brushy, undercut banks and shadowy lies.

Brown Trout Natural History

Knowing a little about the life of browns is at once interesting and worthwhile from an angling perspective. Robert Behnke (whose books are listed in the "Further Reading" appendix) is the best in the world on anything related to trout natural history.

Brown trout are native to Europe, northern Africa, and western Asia. They have been widely introduced to almost all parts of the world, and are currently found in most of the United States, southern Canada, South America, and New Zealand. They were introduced to the Madison River in Montana in 1889 and are now found in most of western and central Montana.

The fish spawn in the fall, usually between October and December. Males and females move up tributary streams to spawn. Females dig a shallow nest, or redd, in the gravel. The eggs are deposited in the redd and take about fifty days to hatch. Young brown trout become sexually mature after two to five years. In Europe and Chile some populations of brown trout are called anadromous because they feed and grow in the ocean, and swim up tributaries in the fall to reproduce. In these populations females develop very slimy skin, probably to protect them when they dig their redds. The males, on the other hand, develop very thick, tough skin.

Brown trout can grow to be quite large, especially sea-run fish. Fish weighing up to 68 pounds have been recorded in Europe, and a specimen weighing 28.5 pounds was caught in Newfoundland.

Brown trout prefer cool, clear rivers and lakes with temperatures of 54 to 66 degrees Fahrenheit. They are wary and elusive fish that look for cover more than any other salmonid. In running waters they hide in undercut banks, midstream debris, surface turbulence, rocks,

East-of-the-Mississippi fly fisher Forrest Glover's father, Gary, landed this enormous river-run brown using techniques Glover describes later in the book.

Brown trout fry are aggressive and establish territories soon after they emerge.

and deep pools. They also take shelter under overhanging vegetation. Brown trout are meat eaters (carnivores). They eat insects from water and land and, as their size increases, take larger prey such as worms, crustaceans, mollusks, fish, salamanders, and frogs. Browns spawn in the fall and early winter. In Montana this activity kicks off in late September and runs into December. In addition to water temperature, I'm convinced that the angle of incidence and decrease in duration of sunlight are key triggering factors for spawning activity.

Browns return to the stream where they were born, choosing spawning sites such as spring-fed headwaters, the heads of riffles, or the tails of a pool. Selected sites have good water flow through the gravel bottom. The female uses her body to excavate a nest (redd) in the gravel. She and the male may spawn there several times. A 5-pound female produces about 3,400 golden-colored eggs, each 4 to 5 millimeters in diameter. Females cover their eggs with gravel after spawning, and the adults return downstream. The eggs develop slowly over the winter, hatching in the spring. A good flow of clean, well-oxygenated water is necessary for successful egg development.

After hatching, the young fish (alevins) remain buried in the gravel and take nourishment from their large yolk-sacs. By the time the yolk-sacs are absorbed, water temperatures have warmed to 45 to 54 degrees Fahrenheit. The fish (now known as fry) emerge from the gravel and begin taking natural food. Brown trout fry are aggressive and establish territories soon after they emerge. They are found in quiet pools or shallow, slow-flowing waters where older trout are absent. They grow rapidly and can reach a size of 5 to 6 inches in their first year.

Yearling brown trout move into cobble and riffle areas. Adults are found in still, deeper waters and are most active at night. They are difficult to catch and are best fished at dawn or dusk. Brown trout living

The allure of stalking trophy browns in beautiful surroundings is hypnotic, overpowering.

in streams grow to about 4 pounds, but lake dwellers and sea-run fish grow larger. They mature in their third to fifth year, and many become repeat spawners.

Hypnotic Attraction

My wife, Ginny, is taking a growing interest in fly fishing. Years of photographing our trips to rivers have fueled her interest in catching fish on her own. I've noticed that many of her photographs are now focused on prime holding water. She seems to be subconsciously honing in on where the fish are. And she watches closely when I cast to likely-looking spots as she tries to see how I do things. I've suggested that this is a mistake of honest proportions, but she smiles and continues her observations. In that spirit I try to stay nearby as she works the water and offer advice gained from decades of modest successes and robust failures.

As an example, one early April day on the Stillwater River south of Columbus, Montana, in the time it took Ginny to quickly take photographs of a nice pool, I'd already worked my way 100 feet upstream from where she was taking photos. In another minute or two, as I was in my own world and oblivious to anyone else, this distance grew to 200, and shortly after that I was around the bend fishing a nice-looking corner pocket. When we reconnected I rigged up a 7-foot Prince fly rod with a large Elk Hair Caddis. This was her first outing of the year, so I gave her a refresher in casting a short line. Years ago our friend John Talia had drummed in the need for and methods of mending, so Ginny was soon casting out to a near seam. I suggested that she work the fly to the outside seam.

"Why?" she asked.

"Because any trout on this side of that seam will have seen us by now. On the other side the browns should still be holding," I replied, and we both saw a couple of fish, maybe 15 to 16 inches each, rise with splashes to caddis escaping the surface meniscus.

"You should write a book on this," she said and laughed. Then she looked over at me clearly, giving her suggestion serious consideration, smiled, and worked line out to cover the lower of the two browns . . .

CHAPTER 2

Reading the Water

The fish and I were both stunned and disbelieving to find ourselves connected by a line.

—William Humphrey, *The Armchair Angler*

Of all the aspects of catching trophy brown trout (or any other trout for that matter) that are discussed in this book, the most important concerns reading water—knowing, or having a very good idea, where large fish are holding or feeding based on the character of the surface. Brilliant casting of the right pattern presented in a cautious, accurate, stealthy manner means absolutely nothing if the water is devoid of trout or contains only smaller fish. Big browns hold in specific locations for very good reasons, including shelter, a steady supply of food, and quality, well-oxygenated water.

Out of a sense of stubbornness bordering on perversity, I once spent several months fishing only a #10 tan Elk Hair Caddis in what I knew to be holding areas for big browns. Many of the places were perfect for Woolly Buggers, nymphs, smaller Humpies, and soft hackles, but I wanted to prove to myself that presentation and location were more important than pattern selection.

Big browns are secretive, predacious, and a true challenge for all of us.

I realize that fishing in Montana is far different than fishing the limestone creeks of Pennsylvania or the mountain streams of the Catskills, but I discovered that I took nearly as many large trout—browns, Yellowstone cutthroats, rainbows, and brook trout—using this one fly in one size as I did when I used all of the dozen-plus patterns I normally use. And when I was fishing in Wisconsin a few years back, I tried the same experiment with similar results. Years ago I watched Tom Rosenbauer drive trout crazy at DePuy's Spring Creek south of Livingston with a large Woolly Bugger while other fishermen using matching patterns had little success. Tom is a master at reading water and proved this to me with his Bugger demonstration on the highly selective water of DePuy's. He was laughing the whole time, while I kept a wary eye out for purists packing heat. None materialized, but a few bad looks were fired our way.

Types of Holding Water

I've identified a dozen basic kinds of holding water. While there are infinite variations on most of these, the basic angling methods for each will handle the often-slight differences. Recognizing and understanding these basic water types will cover any situation encountered on a river and lead to an increase in the number and size of browns landed. Others may divide these differently or lump some of them together, but this breakdown works for me from the perspective of recognition and simplicity. I'll also discuss situations on spring creeks, since they often provide a graduate course on the following holding water types. The twelve are:

1. Riffles
2. Runs
3. Pools
4. Midstream obstructions
5. Undercut and sheltered banks
6. Current seams
7. Streambed depressions
8. Overhead cover
9. Artificial bank structure
10. Eddies
11. Corners
12. Buckets

Riffles

Riffles are often the most productive portions of any river. The rushing water is well oxygenated (a prime big trout requirement) and the rapid flow washes a steady stream of food—including nymphs, dead surface insects, and minnows—to waiting fish. That said, I've taken far more large rainbows and cutthroats than hefty browns in this type of habitat. The main reason for this seems to be that when browns reach around 18 inches they become largely piscavorious, feeding on forage fish and even their own kind to the near exclusion of more conventional food sources. The current normally found in riffles is too strong for the smaller fish preferred by big browns: the dace, sculpins, and chubs. Survival for these smaller fish requires staying in calmer waters found near banks or in pools and flats.

The times I've connected with big browns have been in low-light conditions found at dawn and dusk or on overcast days. I took the fish on large nymphs like #8 to #10 Princes or on streamer patterns, especially sculpins or dace imitations. This seems to indicate that the browns are risking exposure from above-water predators to take advantage of the large, easily taken supply of stonefly nymphs, small trout, or minnows being washed from upstream.

Whenever I encounter riffles, even shallow ones of less than a foot, I look for specific fish to target. Browns are particularly easy to spot as they feed in swift side-to-side searching motions in the current. I have not seen them scrounge for nymphs like other species (nymphing rainbows will often root around in the streambed cobble with their snouts, tails flashing above the surface). Browns seem to prefer concentrating on food washed down to them by the current or attacking smaller fish that have strayed in the paths of a feeding brown.

Riffles, even shallow ones, are solid holding water for browns that will take nymphs throughout the season.

Brown trout take no prisoners when feeding or defending territory.

When selecting a streamer pattern, I prefer larger flies on a 7-foot leader tapered to 3X to 4X. I don't use any weight at the head of the pattern. The weight of the streamer itself is sufficient for this situation. The larger size attracts the fish I'm seeking. Anything scared off is probably not of the size I'm interested in.

One time I spotted browns slashing through the water on a riffled side channel of the Yellowstone above Columbus. The riffle ranged from 1 to 2 feet deep. Mixed among the whitefish, rainbows, and Yellowstone cutthroats feeding on stonefly nymphs, I located several browns of 4 pounds and greater. Initially I thought they were feeding on the same food source as the other fish, but then I spotted a couple of dead sculpins in the still water by the bank. Each had a large chunk taken out of its belly, the horseshoe shape of a brown's bite clearly visible, along with teeth marks near the dorsal fins. Brown trout take no prisoners when feeding or defending territory. I tied on a #4 Black-Nosed Dace, waded out to the edge of the broken water, and spotted a brown working back and forth in the current, scattering the other trout as he worked the area. I cast the Dace about 20 feet upstream and maybe 10 feet beyond the big trout, giving the streamer plenty of time to sink the short distance to the bottom. Then, as the imitation neared the brown, I began to impart life to it with short, erratic strips. Within seconds my quarry spotted the Dace, raced toward it, and took it in a wide-open crunching attack. I lifted the rod, and the brown raced downriver; he was soon into the reel's backing. The fish sounded in a deep pool and eventually tired. It was 25 inches, heavy, and still flashing the silvery shades of summer instead of the honey browns of autumn spawning.

After releasing this one, I went back upstream and took several more browns, all over 20 inches, and one large Yellowstone cutthroat. Nearly every cast of the large Black-Nosed Dace scattered the rainbows and cutthroats. The size probably terrified them. The mountain whitefish would briefly scatter in a flurry of confusion before returning in a moment, first to examine my fake and then to resume their feeding on the abundant supply of nymphs.

Where big browns are concerned, they mainly use riffles as sources for feeding on smaller prey in the form of forage fish and little trout. Look for their swift movements and cast a large streamer well above them.

Runs

The biggest browns I've caught in my life have come from pools and runs in roughly equal numbers. A classic brown trout run reminds me, to some extent, of a pool. It is deep, dark, and full of mystery. You think, "How big a fish is down there?" It is often too deep and swift to wade across.

Runs often begin at the tail end of both pools and riffles, anywhere water gathers in volume and then shoots downstream, running free. The depth can be anywhere from a foot or so up to 8, 9, or 10 feet. These stretches on large western rivers can cover the length of a football field and be maybe a dozen feet wide. On a number of my favorite central Montana rivers, the best runs cut beneath grassy, brushy, tree-lined banks. They are usually 50 feet or less, 4 or 5 feet deep, and free of subsurface obstructions like limbs, large rocks, or snarls of barbed wire.

These prime holding areas are easy to spot, even from well downstream as an angler works his way upriver. Lighter water near one bank gradually darkens as it crosses the stream course and gains in depth. The color is frequently deep aquamarine or dark sapphire. The surface is normally smooth or marked by gentle ripples of current that pulse like waving strands of vegetation in a spring creek.

Depending on the season or time of day, large trout can hold in the calmer, benthic currents along the streambed. Here they feed easily on large nymphs or careless minnows, including sculpins, a

Deep runs in rivers are prime locations for trout, especially in the heat of summer when cool, well-oxygenated water is at a premium.

species whose flattened shape helps it hug the bottom even in moderate current. Streamers and large nymphs are used here. When larger nymphs begin to work their way to the surface—nymphs like caddisflies and stoneflies (or, in the East, mayflies)—browns will ascend the water column, following this activity. Nymph and emerger patterns are the best choices. When the activity is on the surface, large dries work best for the big browns. Smaller flies may take more fish, but they also take mostly smaller fish. When no activity is seen or expected, searching with a streamer is the best option as opposed to nymphing. Streamers tend to provoke either a feeding or territorial response from reluctant browns where nymphs will often be ignored, even after dozens of drifts through the same run. When grasshoppers are present, the browns will line up along these runs, especially those next to grassy banks, snapping and gorging on the large, careless hoppers.

   With runs think big—both with patterns and in the size of trout.

Pools

No other type of stream habitat attracts the eye of a fly fisher like a deep, aquamarine pool fed by a seam of white, bubbling water—a structure resembling a miniature lake, often with little or no noticeable current, finally giving way to a shallow tongue of smooth water that pours into a whitewater riffle or a deep seam of dark current.

   While I caught many trout, large and small, in pools during my first forty years of fishing, it wasn't until I took the time to sit down or stand on the bank and carefully study a number of pools on rivers and creeks (including the North Fork of the Flathead, Spotted Bear, Big Spring Creek, and the Yellowstone) that I came to realize that I was not reading the water effectively or even correctly in many instances.

   Most times I would wade halfway up a pool and began launching my flies—dries, nymphs, streamers—into the rushing water at the head of the pool, allowing the pattern to run down through the heart of the stream before swinging out in the shallows. I often spotted trout, both large and small, moving toward the far bank, upstream, or into deeper water. I rightly assumed that in most of these cases I was watching not just spooked but horrified trout fleeing for cover at my audacious approach.

After four years of doing as much observing as fishing—something not easy to do given the innate call to cast, Cast, CAST!—I discovered that I was making a number of fundamental, strategic mistakes. The first was not fishing the shallow tail-out of a pool, water I frequently neglected entirely. Casts of anywhere from 25 to 50 feet, depending on the size of the water, were required. These casts needed to be made while I was downstream, preferably located behind a jutting bank or a tangle of limbs, or even on my knees. The browns were often large, especially during low-light conditions, and they were mostly hunting down small fish. To avoid scaring the browns, I needed to cast a streamer well away from the fish, let it sink to the bottom, and then begin my retrieve. In this shallow, clear water, visibility was excellent, and the trout would often see my pattern and rush to attack. When fish were present in these tongues, I'd take one and sometimes two browns, but rarely more as the ensuing struggle would drive away other fish.

The next mistake appears ridiculous to my eyes now. Instead of working methodically up through the pool, starting close and gradually casting farther toward the far bank like a reasonably sane, competent angler, I'd fire a cast to the top of the pool into what I observed to be the prime drift. In the process I scared off most of the good browns. Now I measure my casts, adjusted to the size of the water, and cast upstream slowly, working my casts across the pool. The first cast is directly upstream with the angle moving toward quartering (or even straight across if fishing with a streamer), then farther away from me. My success rate both in numbers and size more than doubled.

When fishing beneath the surface in a pool, I also learned to make sure that whatever pattern I was using had ample opportunity to sink to the bottom, often through a dozen feet or more of water, thoroughly drifting on whatever currents were spinning and twisting down below. With experience I learned to control line with subtle, slight retrieves that avoided bellying of line and also created artificial movement in the streamer or nymph. This sometimes took as long as a minute or more. Then I'd begin a retrieve that mimicked a forage fish working its way up the water column and toward the safety of bank-side shallows and cover. Big browns would sometimes hammer my fly after what I'd already considered a fruitless drift. The hits were so vicious that I now use 3X or even 2X tippet to cut down on break-offs. Recently on small, almost hot tub–size pools, I dredged up a number of good browns after allowing the streamer to swim along the bottom for close to a minute.

> With experience I learned to control line with subtle, slight retrieves that avoided bellying of line . . .

Finally, I failed to notice that trout often hold in relatively shallow water at the end of a stretch of fast water, before the current digs and drops down into the heart of the pool. These holding areas are often so thin, maybe 6 inches, that I found it hard to believe that fish of several pounds would or could stay in these diminutive locations. Dozens of fish later, I now know better. I'd always fished the drop-offs and ignored working a cast that would run through these pockets of shallow water. My friend John Talia offered a solid observation on the subject: "I have found many big browns living in tail-outs of runs during the day, and my theory on this is that as evening approaches, they will begin moving up into the run to feed on small fish that are completely unsuspecting of the upcoming stealth attack. Accordingly, before the sun hits the water, in the dim light of morning and evening, streamers are incredibly effective. Let's face it—they are true predators . . ."

Pools now mean slowing down, observing, and defining a strategy that covers the water while avoiding spooking fish as much as possible.

Pools are one of the most obvious places to find big browns, but often some of the toughest places to fish.

The process is enjoyable, too. I've noticed more deer, otters, red-tailed hawks, marten, etc., than ever before. One of the main reasons I fish is to enjoy the natural world. Slowing down intensifies this experience.

Midstream Obstructions

Midstream obstructions can be anything from boulders the size of 1951 four-door Buicks or stranded cottonwoods resembling gigantic corpses to an object as innocuous as a fence post.

Trout are creatures of opportunity. What may seem to us like little or nothing in terms of cover and protection from predators turns out to be a mansion in the pea-size brain of a brown. I've taken browns of 3 pounds on the Little Blackfoot in western Montana, which are large fish for this stream, using nothing more than a #12 Elk Hair Caddis cast sidearm beneath sagging strands of rusting barbed wire and next to a metal fence stake less than 2 inches wide. A brown was parked less than a foot behind this holding in a gravel depression caused by current swirling around the metal. I've caught four browns over the years at this same stake; the smallest was 15 inches.

Boulders parked in the middle of rivers are easy targets. Casting a large dry fly 6 feet above them and letting it bob past often takes enormous fish, either in the calm water caused by hydraulics in front or in the pocket behind. Streamers and nymphs running the same route work as well.

Boulders and large rocks also create pocket water—those mini pools lying just below falling, rushing water. They are excellent spots to fish; "picking pockets" it's often called. Cast just above them and then from a side angle that allows the fly to drop into the hold and doesn't spook the trout. The float will be short, but it never hurts to allow some extra time so a dry fly will spin around on the surface or a nymph will dredge the bottom of the pocket.

Often a good fish is sitting directly behind these obstructions and will not move to either side to take a fly. Cast the fly above and

Midstream obstructions like this jumble of logs, limbs, rock, and gravel create
excellent holding water, both above and below.

beyond the rock and mend line so that the line drags the fly and drops it, plop, in the trout's pocket. The trout will take quickly, as food in these spots moves out of range in an instant, swept away by rapid currents. This is fortunate for the angler because drag on the line will allow no more than a foot or so of drag-free float. The fish's necessarily quick decision to take eliminates the exposure of the pattern as a fake. All the same, allow the fly to finish its float below the boulder even if it is dragging. Big fish will often turn and chase the fly out of predatory instinct. And there are times when the water swings around the rock and pushes upstream so the brown is facing downstream, contrary to normal holding direction.

Fishing bridge abutments needs a slightly different tactical approach. The best bet is to work as much in front of the abutment as possible so that casts can be placed to either side. Obviously, dragging a fly over this type of obstruction is impossible. And there are times when the current is too strong and deep to work the far side. All I can say is do your best on the available portion of the structure and move on. Streamers and nymphs worked down deep also seem to far outperform dry flies. The same approaches also apply to wooden fence posts, even when they are submerged. Hooks have an uncanny way of embedding in wood, especially sodden wood.

Midstream obstructions are targets of random opportunity, but always worth a few casts.

Undercut and Sheltered Banks

Undercut and sheltered banks are my favorite habitat for taking large browns. They almost always are located on scenic stretches of a river, their varied structures present a challenge, and along with pools are the best big-fish holding water around.

The upper Clark Fork River above Deer Lodge, Montana, offers stretches where dense clumps of willow and alder lean over banks that are covered with thick mats of native grass. The river is less than

20 feet wide in places as it twists and turns its way toward Missoula. Each bend is undercut from the gouging force of the moving water. I've pushed a 7-foot rod far back beneath some of the banks here. This sheltered darkness is the home of really big browns. They are safe from the predations of hawks, eagles, and small mammals, along with most humans, and food comes to them in abundance in this rich water. Because they feel safe, it's not as difficult to entice these big browns into striking as one might initially think. While big fish in the open tend to keep to a narrow, well-defined area, the fish under banks will roam from side to side seeking food. They are acutely aware of any sizable food source drifting by just beyond the undercut or outside the shelter of overhanging branches, exposed roots, or grass.

There is a quarter mile of water in this stretch, and that afternoon I caught and released more than thirty browns . . .

One hot July afternoon, walking through a field to my favorite spot on this section of the river, I kicked up thousands of clacking grasshoppers. The bugs were large, so I tied on a #6 and began fishing my way upstream. My first casts were okay, perhaps a foot or so from the bank, but there were no takers. I was being too tentative, too cautious, afraid to break off a Joe's Hopper in the brush. Finally I began slamming the flies tight to the bank, sometimes skipping them off the water's surface into the bank itself, where they plopped back into the water. Immediately I started catching fish. There is a quarter mile of water in this stretch, and that afternoon I caught and released more than thirty browns, ranging from 14 inches up to several pounds. There are bigger fish in this run, but not many.

When I put the hopper tight to the bank, I caught fish. Six inches away and nothing. On other rivers working similar habitat, and using streamers or nymphs rather than hoppers, the results are always the same. On one river in mid-October, I was casting Woolly Buggers along a long run of undercut bank that was draped with thick, browning grass, roots and limbs, and clumps of willow and alder. I needed to throw the Bugger sidearm to slice it beneath the overhanging tangles. When my casts came up short, even by 8 inches or so, I would not see a fish. When I put it onto the bank and dragged it into the river or slammed it tight to the undercut, the browns would shoot out and grab the pattern then immediately try to run to cover. Often at the bite of the hook they'd leap through the tangles of grass, limbs, and roots in order to snap my tippet.

One brown of several pounds did this three times in one fall. The next season I tied on 1X tippet just for him, hoping he was still alive and around. My first cast and my second came up well short. The third rammed into the bank above where I hoped he was holding and sank quickly. Before I could even begin stripping line, he hammered the Bugger and went to the air, tail-walking into thick grass and some flexible willow branches. I literally yanked him a couple of feet out into the river, where I fought him for ten minutes as he ran downstream from small pool to small pool before tiring. He measured 25 inches against my rod and around 14 inches in girth, which equated to 6 pounds—one of the largest ever for this river for me. Once again the need for bank-tight casts was emphatically brought home.

These undercut banks may border water that, in the low flows of late summer and early autumn, is less than a foot deep. I've caught fat browns in water so thin that their dorsal fins, back, and tail fins were exposed to the air. But there are always spots of sufficient depth under the banks, especially near where small, dripping springs come into the river. These spots will hold some of the largest browns in any river. The key is to be willing to lose flies on bank debris. How long does it take to tie or purchase another Yellow Humpy? How long will you remember a 23-inch brown?

As Gary LaFontaine said to me years ago on the Little Blackfoot River one summer evening, "Plan on losing some flies along here. Maybe a lot of flies. If you don't throw the fly into the bank beneath the bushes, all you'll catch are little fish."

Current Seams

Current seams are often keys to locating big trout. Where a river's separate channels blend into a well-defined strip of water, there will be fish waiting for a steady delivery of food, either in the form of aquatic insects, terrestrials, or minnows sucked into the faster current. These strands of current also distort light, creating a form of shelter from avian predators like herons and eagles. Sometimes several seams will line up like undulating serpents, stretching from one bank to the other; this can happen even in smaller streams of 20 feet. On relatively level stretches of a stream course, the seams are often difficult to locate, particularly when the streambed is smooth and the substrate does not disrupt the flow.

One of the easiest and surest ways of finding a current seam is to look for a foam line. Moving water tumbles and spins, and even if these motions are minor, the action of liquid mixing with air creates collections of bubbles that mark the current seam as clearly as a street sign. With more vigorous current, this foam may be a steady stream that runs for dozens of yards downstream. Foam lines are also key locators in pools that may otherwise appear featureless from a current perspective.

Big browns will often work both sides and the middle of these situations, moving easily to suck in nymphs or other food as it is washed by. The temptation is to cast into the mix of foam, especially when the large snouts of gorging browns are clearly visible in the off-white bubbles. But the best way to approach foam lines is to cast your dry, emerger, nymph, or occasionally a streamer to the near edge and work a drag-free drift well below the casting position. Do this several times before repeating the process through the middle of the foam. In dry fly fishing, using the largest pattern you feel you can get away with both helps get a big brown's attention and makes for better visibility. This is one of the main reasons I prefer bulky, high-floating patterns like an Elk Hair Caddis, Humpy, or Adams. Finally, cast along the outside edge of the foam line, doing everything possible to avoid

Foam lines are clearly visible indications of feeding lanes that should be worked from the inside edge, then in the foam, and finally along the outside edge.

drag, including holding the rod high and parallel to the water's surface while lightly mending line to adjust to slight variations in current. Leaning over toward the outer edge will gain a foot or more of precious control.

When foam lines aren't present, watching where leaves, grass, sticks, and dead insects float serves the same purpose. In this case, the seam should be worked as above.

Another good spot for big fish is the V-shaped patch of smooth water above where two or more channels rejoin after having been split by an obstruction in the stream. Tossing a large nymph or streamer a dozen feet above the point of the V and stripping in line rapidly to gain and maintain line control will potentially turn a big trout. The current in these places is sufficiently strong to preclude smaller fish, but more than acceptable for sizable trout. I cast into such a structure in late August last year on a river not far from town. On three consecutive casts I took a brown, a rainbow, and a brown, each from 17 to 21 inches. How these three adult fish managed to get along together is a mystery. I can only think that the abundance of food in a somewhat calm holding area eliminated internecine disputes.

Watching a river flow for a while will allow your eyes to adjust to the conditions. Eventually subtle twists and variations in water movement will reveal themselves and the current seams they represent. As always, fish these in the three steps described above—inside, middle, outside.

I prefer floating lines when working most water, including current seams. I have better control and visibility of both the line and, by direct extension, the fly I'm using. I adjust the depth by throwing upstream mends for slack, allowing the pattern to sink. I also add weight when necessary. In really deep, swift stretches, I might use a sink tip of 6 feet, something like those designed by Jim Teeny Fly Lines. These get my nymph down where it needs to be. I also prefer a relatively firm rod for subsurface work. This allows better control and doesn't sacrifice much in the way of feel and detection of light takes.

Often the current near a bank is strong enough to make a drag-free drift difficult. In cases like this, depending on the direction of the water's flow, a curve cast can give you a few extra feet (often all it takes to move a fish) of realistic float. A curve cast creates a curve in the leader by whipping the rod tip to the right or left during the end of the power stroke. Curve casts give you an opportunity to present the fly to the fish before the line becomes visible. They can be used to reach a fish holding downstream behind a boulder or to put a fly under

Where two or more seams of current merge, there will usually be big fish holding
on the edges of the turbulence.

an overhang with protective cover. Curve casts are also helpful in casting across faster currents so that the fly presents a longer period of
drag-free drift within the slower water on the other side.

Curve casts can be made to go either right or left. If you are
right-handed, a left curve is the easier one. The rod is stroked with
a sidearm cast on a horizontal plane. Check the rod sharply at the
completion of the forward stroke. The amount of curve will depend on
the extent of the overpower in the forward stroke and how sharply you
check the stroke. Some casters will add a reach to the right at the end
of the stop to increase the inertia effect on the line and deepen the
curve. Another technique, usually used for tighter left curves, is to do
an overhand cast with your arm but sharply twist your hand and wrist
to the left. The rod tip will make a left curve arc which the line follows.

A right curve tends to be more difficult for a right-handed caster.
Bring the rod across your opposing shoulder and deliver an overpow-
ered forward stroke with an abrupt checking stop. The line will reach
the end of its travel and then hook to the right. If you reach to the left
after the stop, you will get a tighter right curve. The other variation to
this cast is to use an overhand forward stroke with your arm but twist
your hand and wrist to the right.

To execute a pile curve cast, bring the forward stroke lightly
upward. The line will hook and arc upward, then drop to the water
surface in a pile. This technique will only work well on windless days
on flat water, and is particularly suited to small dries.

Streambed Depressions

Streambed depressions are one of the least known, least recognized,
and least fished types of big trout holding water. These often slight
scourings in a riverbed can hold tremendous trout, fish that are rarely
disturbed and as a result quite susceptible to an angler's attentions.
It only takes a few inches in depth to provide a holding area for a big
brown. Most rivers hold countless numbers of these depressions.

Up until twenty years ago I was oblivious to these spots until my friend John Talia focused my attention on them while we were seeking out enormous rainbows on the Missouri River below Fort Peck Dam. In the ensuing years John's suggestion lay dormant in a little-looked-at angling file tucked away in the cobwebbed recesses of my mind. But then, one glorious October afternoon, I found myself fishing a side channel on the Yellowstone an hour downstream of Livingston. An enormous cottonwood arced over the smooth water, its leaves flaming yellow against the cloudless blue sky. Forty feet from me I noticed a minor disturbance in the surface of the river, and for some reason flashed "Talia's depression." I cast a #12 Elk Hair a dozen feet above the ripple, allowing for downstream motion of the water to locate the structure. There was just time to make an upstream mend when an enormous splashing take tightened the line. Seconds later a lengthy brown walked across the surface, headed for Billings 60 miles distant. The back-and-forth confrontation lasted for a few minutes, but clear water worked in my favor as the fish tired and came to my feet. Easily 2 feet and 4 pounds, this brown was the first I'd ever consciously taken from a dip in a river's substrate. From then on when fishing smooth stretches of river that have spread out over a gravel or rock shelf, I look for the slight disturbances in the surface that can indicate a holding spot for big fish.

Browns like these locations because they are sheltered from the current and also deliver a steady supply of food. These spots are best when situated close to cover like undercut banks, pools, or logjams. In deep runs browns will hold in these places also because of the protection afforded by several feet of moving water. This is when a large, weighted nymph is the best bet since the trout rarely move to the surface when settled in along the river bottom. In shallow water a dry fly provides excellent sport.

The fish in these dips are usually the largest in a given stretch of river. Dips are near prime cover, depressions are excellent feeding

The darker water just ahead of the moss is a streambed depression that yielded an 18-inch brown on a Yellow Humpy.

stations, and in the territorial world of a brown trout, size does matter. Large, trophy fish hold sway and corner the best seats at the table.

Another plus to streambed depressions is that most anglers, including many guides, overlook these places. Many times the holds are located in what appears to be dead water, leading most drift boats and rafts to rush on by to apparently better pickings. I've seen this happen dozens of times as I stood in 2 feet of water biding my time until a group of fly fishers rowed past amid a flurry of obligatory comments like "Nice day, isn't it?" "How are you doing?" and "Later." As soon as the merry souls are around the bend, physically speaking, I cast to the depression I've located from earlier bank-side walking reconnaissance or have remembered from an earlier experience. When I connect with a trout of several pounds after making a quartering upstream cast of 50 feet, I smile to myself and say a silent thanks to Talia.

Overhead Cover

Overhead cover can consist of anything from low-hanging tree limbs or wooden bridges to a few strands of wire hanging from slouching cedar fence posts. The point of overhanging structure from a brown trout's world view is once again tied to the fact that, like most apex predators (and in a trout stream, that's what brown trout are), they are creatures of opportunity. And overhead cover affords large browns the opportunity to move into a river's otherwise dangerous food-delivery current seams. These are areas where, in the absence of overhead cover, avian predators would have a much easier time making an overhead attack. So even those few strands of limp fence wire give the shelter needed to move out into the river and feed steadily on readily available sources of food like nymphs, emergers, and dries. An eagle can't swoop down on the brown without crashing and entangling itself in the wire. The same is true for many smaller bridges whose proximity to the water's surface prevents large raptors from silently gliding in an snaring trout in their talons. Limbs—same situation.

Working up to, around, and sometimes above these objects and structures often requires sidearm casting while crouched low to the river's surface. Curve casts can help here, too. A right-hand curve cast requires under-powering the forward cast or stopping short of the normal completion arc. Just as the line straightens, pull back the rod tip just enough to stop the fly in its forward path, A left-hand curve needs the angler to overpower the line or, as G. L. M. La Branche wrote, "When the desired distance is reached, 'imagine that the casting line has neither fly nor leader attached to it,' and before the final forward cast has fully extended, prematurely release the line held in the line hand, so that the energy of the cast 'is diverted to pulling out loose line' instead of extending the cast."

> I never ignore cross-stream fence wire or boards. I've taken many good fish from these unlikely locations.

Frequently I've observed swallows and swifts dipping and swooping beneath bridges, feeding on the caddisflies, mayflies, and stoneflies that remain near the water's surface because they are at least partially sheltered from the wind. The browns take advantage of this along with the protection, and feed rather recklessly in these places. Same is true of overhangs. The fish appear to believe themselves invincible from attack by marauding raccoons, martens, and herons, so casting is made easier.

I never ignore cross-stream fence wire or boards. I have taken many good fish from these unlikely locations. This holds true for all overhead shelter, but the strands of wire hold my fascination because initially one would think that something so slight would have no effect on a large fish's behavior.

This stately cottonwood sheltered a slight streambed depression that yielded a nice brown on an Elk Hair Caddis.

Artificial Bank Structure

One of the attractions of fishing is the way it gives us a chance to interact with the natural world. So it is understandable when many of us pass by man-made structures along a river and ignore their opportunities. Who wants to fish a stream course that resembles the L.A. River? In doing this, we may also be passing up the big browns who, as always, opportunistically take advantage of any quality holding water. Whether concrete chunks used as riprap, rock and gravel used in the same way, or even embedded car bodies, these bank-side "improvements" are rarely pleasant to look at but may translate into excellent cover, habitat, and holding water.

There are several sections of bank stabilized with large chunks of concrete along the Bitterroot River in southwestern Montana. Over the years friends and I have taken plenty of large browns from the pockets, holes, and miniature caves formed by this material. Many times big streamers pull the browns out. At other times, like during the Skwala stonefly hatch in March, big bushy dries are gulped by not only large browns, but equally big rainbows and cutthroats. I've had browns tug line back into a dark hole and break off by abrading the leader against the rough surface of the concrete. Many times it is the most productive water on a river on a given day, often because it does not receive as much attention from anglers as other types of water do.

The classic Montana bank-improvement structure is a series of rusted-out 1940s and 1950s Buicks, DeSotos, Packards, and Dodge pickups. This material is now outlawed, but I'm sure that, over the decades, thousands of trout have been dragged from the security of their backseat hideaways by fly fishers. I know one gaggle of cars on a western Montana river where I've taken at least a dozen browns of 3 to 6 pounds on hoppers in the summer and Woolly Buggers in the fall. Those cars also hold a bunch of my flies and tippet material. Whenever I spot an old car decaying on a riverbank, partially submerged, with cool, clear water flowing in through its windshield and out the window

I've forgotten how many browns I've pulled out of old, rusted cars over the years.

openings, I think, "Oh boy, Holt. Here's some easy pickings for a big brown." Surprisingly, this holds true more than half the time.

I prefer natural habitat, but I'm not going to cut off my nose to spite my face when it comes to artificial structure and fishing for big browns.

Eddies

The operative dictum for this type of stream structure is, "Whenever you see an eddy, fish it." No questions asked. This is prime big trout water.

Wherever water spins along the edge of a river's main downstream flow, there are fish. The only exception I can think of is if beavers have decided to make their mud and limb lodges alongside an eddy. Even then, trout will often resettle once the mammalian construction and related mayhem has died down.

Eddies are easy to identify by their whirlpool, galaxy-like appearance. They are often covered in foam, the stuff so dense at times that it stacks up in clumps several inches tall. Beneath this spinning water wait the trout, big ones who hold patiently on the edges and down at the base, feeding on a variety of food sources, including the usual insect suspects and forage fish. Sometimes small frogs or rodents fall into the water and are sucked down into the maelstrom.

Obtaining a decent drift in an eddy is difficult but not impossible. Often the fish are facing upstream, into the bank or toward the angler, depending on the disposition of the eddy. Browns face into the current, but this does not mean always upriver. Taking a few moments to thoroughly observe a particular eddy will translate into fish instead of frustration. It is possible to wade quite close to these structures. And while your cast may only drift naturally for a foot or two, this is plenty of distance. The trout are conditioned to strike swiftly at any food source offered in an eddy, especially when they're hiding under foam, losing much of their wariness.

La Branche wrote nearly one hundred years ago about making as many as a dozen casts trying for only a couple feet of good drift. He

Eddies are revolving carousels that bring food to fish holding in this water. The fish will face against the current, which often means looking downstream. Eddies require a thoughtful approach.

wasn't concerned about putting down the trout, reasoning the abundance of food and the security provided by the foam cover kept big fish feeding aggressively.

I've had only sporadic success allowing my fly to swing out of the spinning water and unnaturally along the edge and on downstream. Eddies offer so much food that anything acting outside the norm will be rejected, at times with a greater refusal rate than on the smooth flats (where trout are expected to be highly selective). As always, work the water closest to your wading position and gradually fish away from you toward the far bank, where the largest brown is often holding.

I now drop a large, #6 or #8 Prince in the middle of thick foam like manna from heaven, reaching and leaning as far as possible. I've overreached to the extent that I've had a ride in the river, trying to gain every last inch of drift. A rod of at least 8'6" or 9'0" helps. These nymphs are tied weighted, and I often attach one or two split shot at the head. Bead heads work as well, but for as yet undefined and I'm sure arcane reasons, I don't like to use these. I guess I prefer being able to adjust the split shot, where sometimes it is advantageous to move them a couple of inches above the fly. The choice is yours.

Corners

Corners are where a river's current turns, creating an inside area of relatively calm water that often resembles a pool. These structures are usually shallower than the main flow, and are excellent holding areas for trout during times of insect activity. Big fish also move into these locations at dusk and work the shallows relentlessly until dawn, tearing through schools of minnows.

Corners are especially advantageous for the wading angler. Where much of a river might only be reachable by floating, corners offer the opportunity for the bank fisher to work some of a large river's most productive water. Cast directly across or nearly dead upstream.

Steady and rapid stripping is necessary for line control. Maintaining contact with the fly during a drag-free float is crucial, otherwise many takes will be missed due to slack. The brown will take and then reject or slip the hook in the space of inches.

As always, working from inside out to the main flow is the best approach. On some days when I'm in a patient frame of mind, I'll work a corner pocket with a dry, then a nymph, and finally a streamer. I usually expect to have driven off the trout by the time I reach the last approach, but have surprised myself with large fish on the streamer. Apparently the browns were not interested in or frightened by the smaller dries and nymphs.

Buckets

Buckets are pools in the flow of the river, formed by drops in the streambed. When floating, they are spotted by an abrupt drop in current near the bank, patches of deeper, smoother water next to the turbulence of the main flow.

A skilled guide will point these out and position his raft to come in from the outside, allowing the caster time and a good angle to hit the water. This is precise, rapid-fire fishing for those big trout that have moved into these places for the abundant food and the proximity to shelter offered by adjacent deep water. It can be both frustrating and extremely productive fishing. Some of my friends who are both superb guides and casters laugh out loud at my bungling, inept attempts to rapidly adjust from a bank-side run to a quick shot into the bucket. When drifting, dry flies are mostly used. When I'm wading, I'll sometimes plop a nymph into the bucket as well.

As opposed to drifting, the wading angler has time to make a careful, spot-on cast. Look for an angle that allows both a smooth drift and the leader to hit the water without lining the quarry. A directly upstream cast sometimes works, but is definitely a one-shot affair.

Just inside the broken water right below the point of the limb, a "bucket" held a nice brown.

Observation Is Key

As with most aspects in life, patience is the key to success. Take the time to really see what is taking place before your eyes. When it comes to reading water, consider what structures are present, how the current or currents are acting and interacting, and where the big fish might be holding. Once the variables are taken into account, formulate a strategy of approach, technique, leader length, and fly pattern. The patient, observant angler is the successful angler. For my part, whenever I find myself moving too quickly, I tell myself, "Slow down! What's the hurry?"

CHAPTER 3

The Surface Game

Never throw a long line when a short one will serve your purpose.
—Richard Penn, ca. 1863

The water bubbled and glided, soft and cool along the far bank. In the last week of September, the tall grass flickered gold-brown in the breeze. It had been a wet year, and this was one of the few times my angling partner Jake and I had been able to fish this river.

Our timing was good. It was a windy day, and warm for the time of year. Instead of holding down deep and skulking around in dark holes like outlaw thugs, eating the occasional stray sculpin or caddis nymph, large, hungry brown trout were up all over the place, holding close to the banks, waiting for breeze-blown grasshoppers to come their way.

In less than an hour we'd already landed a half-dozen trout between 18 and 22 inches. We were using ragged versions of a Joe's Hopper, a tragic combination of Cree hackle, antelope hair, rusty gold Antron dubbing, and a sprig of red cut from an old flannel shirt. The hopper looks like hell, but it works. As Jake often says, "Artistic flies catch small, cute fish. Big, ratty bugs take big, ugly browns. Take your pick."

We were also using an obvious and rough-hewn method that Jake likes a lot, one he learned from an old guide named Yellowstone Jack on the Gallatin more than twenty-five years ago. On windy days (a common occurrence out here in the West), as the hopper or large Elk Hair Caddis or Humpy reaches the end of its ride, he allows the line to be buffeted about by the wind, causing the fly to dance and skitter across the surface. Large trout, especially when larger species of caddis like the October version (Trichoptera: Limnephilidae Dicosmoecus, for the masochistic among us) are present, will crash across the surface in mad chase, jaws chattering. The take is so severe, it often leads to snapped tippets.

I watched a big brown attack Jake's fly within 3 feet of the start of a drift. Jake set the hook and played the fish as it sounded along the bronze-colored cobble. The fish rattled its head in anger and then reached for the sky in a series of silver-spray leaps. Each time the brown went to the air, Jake maintained a firm connection with the fish and backed downstream a step or two. By the time the 3-pound trout came to his feet, both angler and fish were well below the run and the other browns were back to feeding. Jake admired the almost spectral gold, bronze, copper, black, white, and red of the large wild brown, and then turned the fish loose.

"That's what it's all about, buddy," he said, and moved a bit upriver to take another fish.

Because of an ill-defined sense of honesty and disclosure, I'm forced to admit that when it comes to fishing for big brown trout, the majority of my time is spent working patterns beneath the surface. And while my admission undoubtedly casts my lot with boorish, crude cohorts in the eyes of many, these ruffians are my people and I embrace them with the fervor of an escaped political prisoner.

As much as 90 percent of a trout's diet is underwater, so it seems prudent to fish down there. I first came across this information when

Big browns, like most big trout, feed mostly on sub-surface food sources; that's why a Woolly Bugger took this guy.

reading Ernie Schwiebert's *Nymphs,* as the author referenced observations by nymph angler extraordinaire Frank Sawyer. And while there are times when big browns work the surface, during certain hatches or when terrestrials are on the water, and times when casting a dry fly is not only the logical approach but the *only* approach to the water, these times seem few and far between. The majority of the big fish I've caught on rivers like the Madison, Bighorn, Big Hole, Missouri, and Beaverhead—except during the crane fly time of the year—have been on large streamers and, to a lesser degree, nymphs.

Having said this, the slight sip of a mayfly, a splashing caddis take, or the gluttonous gulping in of a salmon fly excite me in a way that no other form of fly fishing can. The visual and audio portions of the process are unique in fly fishing. And there are times, often on lazy summer and early autumn afternoons, when I enjoy watching an Elk Hair Caddis or an Adams ride the currents and spin around in eddies. The sight of this carefree voyage is pleasing in an innocent way. Any trout taken are a bonus, often a startling one.

I'm not cut out to be one of the skilled souls that ply their trade on streams like the Henry's Fork or spring creeks when these waters are in a finicky frame of mind. To each his own. I catch my share of large trout doing things in my sometimes addled, search-and-destroy way. The rare times when I actually practice delicate artifice with a long, light leader and small fly like a #20 BWO and manage to succeed make me feel accomplished as a dry fly fisher, but I know better. I'm one of fly fishing's unwashed, and pretending otherwise is folly, self-deception, and a waste of time.

More than eighty years ago, Samuel G. Camp wrote his wonderfully informative yet succinct *Taking Trout with the Dry Fly.* In this work, he quotes from G. P. R. Pulman's *Vade-Mecum of Fly-Fishing for Trout,* which was published in 1846: "It is impossible to give infallible directions for the use of particular flies at every particular time . . . Much must be left to the angler's own judgment; but we advise him to be

This is designer dry fly water for big browns.

careful of falling into the error of constantly changing his flies when fishing, thereby perplexing himself, and, generally speaking, wasting time."

Camp further quoted Pulman with this: "Fish are proverbially
capricious, and many of their habits, in regard to feeding and otherwise, depend on circumstances which with all our knowledge of natural history, are not understood. The angler, therefore, must not be
too ready to attribute his wants of success at any time to a mistaken

selection of his fly. There are many circumstances to which it may with greater justice be traced."

Many "old masters" such as Skues, along with La Branche, Gordon, Halford, Camp, etc., opted for a simpler-is-better approach. Nymphs, wet flies, Woolly Buggers—these are my staples, but there are times when watching a #6 Joe's Hopper bounce down a run in the path an enormous brown, jaws wide open, has its moments.

Dry Fly Approaches

Driving along a road that parallels a river or creek, or hiking up over a rise and spotting a wild stretch of water, my excitement is often triggered by the sight of a deep, clear aquamarine pool dimpled with rising browns. A swift run or waterfall might define the head of this miniature pond, and frequently a smooth glide or another frothing plunge will mark the downstream boundary. There always seem to be fish in these places, but no other stream type requires as much patience or stealth.

In the long-ago days I'd arrive and fling a hopper along a current seam or a Bugger tight to the bank 40 feet away. But now I've learned to spend time analyzing how to fish a particular pool and what fly to use. My goal is to work the water in an orderly fashion, with the intent of taking one or more large browns. I'm not interested in smaller fish at the head of the pool or chasing mayflies in the shallow water. If no trout are feeding on the surface, I'll usually work a hopper (in season) or perhaps a large Elk Hair Caddis or possibly a Neversink Skater or a Rat-Faced McDougal (in homage to the past, to flies that have taken enormous browns over the years). I'll work from the edge of the pool on over to the bank, making several casts in each lane as I go, and finally a number of bank-tight offerings. If the first couple casts spooked a big brown, so what? A few more can't make things worse and will turn trout that are hunkered down in the shadows of the overhanging grasses, roots, and undercut banks.

I like old-time patterns, and the Rat-Faced McDougal is one of them. According to fly tier Allan Podell, Harry Darbee claimed that he and his wife, Elsie, tied several versions of this style of fly in combinations of color shades. They were unnamed patterns but were placed in the first catalogue they published in the 1930s. "They [the flies] were later to become known, thanks to Judge Wiggens of Middletown, New York, as the Beaverkill Bastard, owing to their somewhat questionable origin from the union of a deer hair bass bug and a large trout fly," said Harry. One evening while Harry and a friend, Percy Jennings, were tying these flies, a young female visitor asked what they were called. Not wanting to offend her sensitivities, she was asked to name the fly, and she said, "I think it's a Rat-Faced McDougal."

Unless the browns have been hammered recently, the big ones rarely spook to the point of totally disappearing in a pool. A #10 or #12 Elk Hair mimics caddis, hoppers, and even crickets and large ants. Long casts with double hauls are unnecessary. Anything over 40 to 50 feet is probably counterproductive. Most of my casts, even on big rivers like the Yellowstone and Jefferson, are less than 40 feet. I prefer to cut the water down to size and fish each segment as though it were a small stream unto itself. The late Jack Gartside showed me how to do this in Boston Harbor years ago as we fished for stripers amid a din of low-flying jumbo jets landing at Logan International Airport, police and fire sirens, car crashes, fistfights, and other forms of ordinary madness. "Look for current seams caused by the tides and any structure within these," he said one morning before dawn. "Fishing for stripers is not all that different from what I do on the Missouri when I come to Montana in the summer. Both out there and here I look for situations that define a piece of water to the point where it becomes analogous to places where I've had success before."

> Unless the browns have been hammered recently, the big ones rarely spook to the point of totally disappearing in a pool.

Every inch of this water along the far bank is dry fly water, although the ideal
pattern would depend on the season and time of day.

Gartside added that constant and often small, subtle mending of the line is necessary to adjust for currents that vary in speed and direction. Sometimes on a river the water will slow or even double back upstream briefly when it runs against boulders, logs, or bank protrusions. At these times a corresponding downstream flick of the line close to the leader is necessary instead of the more common upstream mend. Mending along certain sections of the line is easily learned within a few hours or days on the water. The practice then becomes little more than a second-nature flick of the rod as it is held slightly above parallel with the water's surface, generated by the wrist moving in an upstream or downstream semicircular motion.

Reading the currents on smaller streams is straightforward—holding water and prime runs are clearly visible. On a big river much of the water is too fast and deep to bother with, the exceptions being when huge trout are looking up for large food sources like hoppers, forage fish, or fall caddis. At these times a cast quartering up across the river and then stripped back as fast as possible can turn very big browns. Strikes are often missed by trout and angler alike. Not a pretty method, but variety is spice. However, most times look for seams of calmer current, pools alongside banks and gravel bars, and dips in the streambed. And while the tendency is to always cast bank-tight along rough, scrubby cover, many times big fish move out along runs several feet deep and hold in slight depressions away from tiring currents. They're waiting for big bugs to float past, and will follow them for several feet before sucking them in and then heading right back down to the hold.

When considering how to fish a pool, always stop and think about where big trout will hold. Forget about the small ones unless it's a day where numbers count more than size. A 6-pound brown will set up in the center of a pool, but always on the side nearest to cover and safety. The difference of a half-dozen feet is the difference between being knocked off by predation and survival. I've seen and

A bank-side eddy is an ideal place to work a large dry like an Elk Hair Caddis, Yellow Humpy, or Rat-Faced McDougal.

taken many large fish in the centers of pond-like pools in rivers, but with the exception of dawn and dusk, they've always moved out from an area where bank-side shelter was most accessible.

The swirling, revolving pieces of water that form on the sides of pools are natural delivery belts bringing insects, injured minnows, and nymphs to trout holding on the sides of these liquid spirals or side eddies. I used to make long casts when fishing this type of water, attempting to obtain drifts of 20 to 30 feet. But then I focused on the water, really seeing the hydraulics, and started making casts of 30 feet or less. I was just trying to gain a drag-free drift for even as little as a foot in the best sections of the eddy. Since changing my tactics, the numbers and size of fish have both gone up significantly. Where once I was happy to take a 15-inch Yellowstone cutthroat (and I still am), I now discovered browns of several pounds and more in these eddies.

With browns, and in the majority of instances, the dictum "big flies, big fish" applies. Number 6 to 10 Elk Hairs and bigger hoppers work well, as do Humpies, especially yellow, in #8 or #10. A rod of 9' that handles a 5-weight with authority really helps guide the fly through the zone. Leaders of 6 or 7 feet with 3X tippet are best. I realize that many fishermen prefer 15-foot or longer leaders with 6X or 7X tippets. They enjoy this and it works for them and that's good. But try these setups in the water just described with small patterns, and then try the above method and compare the results. Nevertheless, if you're into self-described "purism," I've no qualms about your approach. We all should dance to our own tune.

Pools, runs, and riffles are often separated by interstitial stretches of water known as flats. This water flows lazily over a bottom made up of small gravel, stone, or even sand or silt, with its surface mirror flat, seemingly lifeless. There are times when insects hatch here or minnows swim about in neurotic schools. At dawn or dusk and on overcast days, browns will move out of holding areas and slice through the terrified forage fish. Any streamer that remotely resembles a fish

This is a typical flat that produces browns in low-light conditions.

will work. Longer casts ahead of the working fish are preferred, with 7-foot leaders tapered to 2X or 3X tippet. This is a form of sight fishing that is straightforward in nature. Big trout moving into these calm areas to feed on moving nymphs and emerging insects is a rare event. Exposure to predators is not worth the risk for the calories obtained from a mayfly. An advantage is the lack of current leading to a lower expenditure of energy reserves. Trout don't think in axiomatic terms, but instinctive behavior provides empiric evidence of its truthfulness. When the trout are feeding, long leaders, small tippets, and flies that approximate the hatch are needed.

When approaching a stretch of flat or smooth water that is several or more feet deep and no fish are working, and if I want to fish with dry flies, I'll tie on a large, #10 or #12 Elk Hair. I'll begin by casting directly upstream 50 feet or so, working the same float several times, and working across the water away from me in 1- or 2-foot increments while giving special attention to any current seams, however slight, and foam lines, even if they are little more than thin collections of froth. Both types of water indicate feeding lanes for big trout. Sometimes a large dry fly pattern drifting overhead a number of times will provoke a big brown to rush up from the depths in a wicked, splashy take that can easily lead to snapped leaders. But still, fishing deeper flats is far more productive with streamers.

I've never been a match-the-hatch person. I believe that if the size and shape are correct, matching attributes like exact color shades, delicate wings, and extended tails is unnecessary. This was borne out when I read works by Skues, Halford, and La Branche, all of whom said essentially the same thing. I've watched a skilled friend of mine take trout after large trout using a #12 Green Humpy whose only passing acquaintance with verisimilitude and matching were sporadic appearances of Yellow Sally stoneflies in which the Humpy matched in size and shape. He only had green-bodied flies with him, so the color match was not in play.

This brown fell for an Elk Hair Caddis in a prairie stream that was less than 10 feet wide.

I catch more and larger browns with fewer patterns. As mentioned earlier, I now rarely use more than eight different fly types, but my success rate is better than I ever experienced when carrying boxes containing dozens of different flies. Less is more. Simple is more enjoyable. Less time selecting and tying on different flies translates to more casts and more time for the fly to spend on the water.

Hoppers are Killers

A slight variation on accepted hopper technique follows, since many times persisting in an upstream cast, dead-drift routine will be marked by failure. Sure, a sedate, bank-tight presentation of one of the hundreds of popular patterns looks fine and proper, the way a terrestrial is supposed to be fished, and watching the bushy things bounce downstream is rewarding for most of us, but in Montana there are a number of individuals with little or no respect for fly-fishing convention. New patterns and techniques are constantly evolving under the intense ultraviolet bombardment of a summer's sun.

All my fishing life I've heard that grasshopper patterns are the stuff of big trout in good numbers, and over the years I became proficient at the upstream, dead-drift hopper two-step. It took a fly fisher as far around the bend as the uniquely talented trout sculptor Powell Swanser to show me the error of my pedestrian ways. Swanser, who lives along the Clark Fork River above Missoula with his wife, Tazun, is the inventor of the little-known-but-somewhat-infamous Outlaw Hopper. He also catches as many browns over 24 inches as anyone I've ever heard of. His creation is a white-and-gray and red-in-places extension of the basic hopper paradigm. The thing is ugly but effective. The late Gary LaFontaine said that the pattern was one of the most deadly stimulator ties he ever used for big fish.

Swanser was good friends with Gary. They spent many hours together fishing the upper Clark Fork. LaFontaine did much to popularize skip-casting hopper patterns tight to banks to draw the murderous attention of big browns through the commotion created on the water's surface by the riotous presentation. Swanser has taken this concept even further out into the ozone.

> In addition to its unique appearance, one of the Outlaw's secrets for success is in its presentation.

In addition to its unique appearance, one of the Outlaw's secrets for success is in its presentation. What follows is a distillation into the pure essence of what fishing the Outlaw Hopper is all about.

In late summer and fall, fishing the Outlaw Hopper through this deep run has produced several browns over 20 inches.

"Presentation . . . ah, yes, I've had my share of ridicule," said Swanser. "The presentation techniques I've worked up for this pattern are what I call 'dirty dancing.' And this is no off-the-wall method but rather a bona fide system that makes this fly produce."

Swanser describes the method using a typical late-summer hopper bank, deep side channel scenario. Using a weight-forward 7-weight line, a 6-foot leader, and 20 inches of 3X or 4X tippet, Swanser will normally bypass the tail of the run and concentrate his efforts up through the head of the run, saying that big browns prefer this structure during hopper season.

The first sidearm cast sets the Outlaw gently along the far bank, quartering or dead across stream with as long a drag-free float as possible. The next cast lands a bit harder, and with a twitch given to the bug every two seconds. On the third cast, if he hasn't moved a big brown by now—a rare situation—he skips the hopper off the water's surface and into the bank, every few seconds pulling it underwater with a strip of a foot or two. If the pattern moves too far out of the feeding lane or foam line, Swanser throws a quick line loop like a downsized roll cast or an exaggerated mend, kicking the Outlaw back into place.

"If a big brown hasn't nailed it by now, I'm out of there! I back out low and careful, slip around, and move to the head of the run. I'm down on one knee, stripping out the line I need, plus 10 feet. Then I flip the bug back into the foam line or bank tight and let the current take the thing downstream."

When the pattern has reached the end of the drift and is hanging in the current, Swanser holds it still for three seconds before initiating a slow, straight, deliberate retrieve upstream through the foam line or along the bank. The second cast is allowed to drift several feet farther downstream and is then retrieved in big, sweeping S curves.

"The third cast is the one that has turned more than one nonbeliever into a disciple of the 'true faith,'" said Swanser. "The fly hits the hole 2 feet down from the foam and it doesn't stop bouncing for some time. I have had 25-inch German browns do a complete cartwheel in the air trying to get their clammy little hands on the Outlaw."

If this fails to draw a response from the big trout, hang a split shot on the tippet and shoot the pattern to the tail of the pool, snapping the rod tip sideways to break the surface tension. Then bring the hopper back with rapid, 18-inch strips. The deer hair and soft hackle lay back against the sides of the body during the retrieve, and the fly will make a complete revolution every three or four strips, creating a good deal of turbulence that imitates a wounded minnow.

"One more cast like this should be enough to either incite a strike or drive the inhabitants to the next river," said Swanser. "If nothing has happened and you are convinced that there's a world record in the hole, clip off the deer hair and pull out all of the tail except for two strands on each side. Leave the split shot in place and toss a high one at the head of the run while throwing a mend in the air. Bounce your new stonefly nymph down the trench right past the big brown's nose. Many times this is what that old, spoiled trout has been waiting for."

All of this sounds like a lengthy and complex procedure, but with practice the routine quickly establishes itself in muscle and cerebral memory. The technique is meant for big trout and has the advantage of imitating not only a grasshopper, but a minnow, an egg-laying stonefly, a stonefly nymph, and a large October caddis. I've seen this approach send terrified browns of 10 to 14 inches running for cover, only to have a 22-inch male charge the next cast in the same stretch.

"The Outlaw Hopper is the John Deere tractor of the fly world," said Swanser. "It may not be the prettiest thing in the hayfield, but you'll never be let down when it's time to harvest the hay. More than once I've tossed the Outlaw into the middle of a PMD hatch with ten village idiots gobbling frantically—locked tight to a #16 image—only to have a 24-inch granddaddy try to slam my big bug into the sunset."

While Swanser's method has proven itself to me over the years (most recently last summer on the smaller rivers of central Montana, where I caught a dozen 20-plus-inchers, one of which was 26), there are also other successful variations on hopper fishing, including using my other favorite, Joe's Hopper. Just because thousands of the madly leaping insects are exploding from the streamside grasses, this does not always translate into brain-dead taking of large browns. Normally a day or longer is needed for the trout to really key into an emerging new food source. Grasshoppers are no exception. Eventually the sights and sounds of the insects splatting, crashing, and drifting overhead prove too much for even the most secretive and recalcitrant trout to resist.

This is true of any change in a trout's diet. The fish are opportunistic by nature. They have to be to survive. And they are also extremely efficient feeding machines. Again, they have to be. If they expend more calories than they take in, the sum total equals loss of weight and energy. To abandon a readily available and consistent food source for a new one, even a big one like hoppers, takes time. Often insect appearances are at best transitory and not worth a brown's efforts. Thousands of years of evolution have established behavior patterns that run on this fact. As La Branche described in *The Dry Fly and Fast Water* almost a century ago, even when a certain hatch has been in progress for several days, he often found it necessary to cast a half-dozen times over the same trout to provoke a response. As hoppers make their initial appearance on a river, large fish will remain tight to their holding areas. A patient individual who knows where a specific big brown is lying can often entice the fish into taking with a false hatch created by making numerous casts over the same location. This works with a number of species, including caddisflies, mayflies, and stoneflies.

All the same, once fish do key into hoppers, the fishing can be fabulous for very big trout that have lost most of their wariness and feeding discernment. Ask any angler to list his best days on the water, and one or more of them will surely be when grasshoppers were leaping and flying with mad abandon and huge trout were devouring them.

But be aware that a stretch of river that was productive last year may now be dead water due to changes in water depth, agrarian management practices by the rancher, or changes in the stream channel. Also, grasshoppers may have eaten vegetation to the ground in one stretch and moved on to another more verdant section the next year, or even the next week. I've seen them eat pipe insulation to bare metal and level a family garden to the point where it looks rototilled. When considering where to hopper fish, look for fields of hay, wheat, alfalfa, and wild grasses.

Due to the free-flying nature of grasshoppers, an angler might conclude that trout are found throughout a river wherever and whenever the insects are present. This is not necessarily the case. Big browns are highly selective of holding areas, needing shelter, a steady food-delivery current, and well-oxygenated water. I've seen good-size rainbows turn from tailing for nymphs in water a foot deep to concentrating on hoppers with not a brown, even a small one, to be found. But moving upstream even a few hundred feet to water that has deep undercut, grassy, or brushy banks, or a run of submerged boulders, may be enough to change the situation.

> Big browns are highly selective of holding areas, needing shelter, a steady food-delivery current, and well-oxygenated water.

Hoppers increase in average size as the season progresses. In May I might use a #10, but by late August I'm down to a #6 or #4. When in doubt, go larger rather than smaller. This may mean substantially fewer trout, but will also translate into much larger fish.

One last thing concerning grasshoppers: Despite their natural buoyancy, using a split shot at the head can help attract a big trout or two in an otherwise small-fish stretch. Grasshoppers can become waterlogged under natural conditions, and sink down to tumble along the bottom where large, wary browns hold safely out of sight and

Trout line up along runs like these to savagely devour windblown grasshoppers.

reach of hawks, herons, martens, and other predators. As Swanser said earlier, the sunken hopper can also imitate a large nymph.

I truly believe that the Outlaw Hopper worked in the hands of an experienced, true believer will catch as many huge browns as any method around, but I also think the same way about a Joe's Hopper and all of the other methods described in this book. One more easy-to-learn approach like Swanser's can't do anything but catch more big fish and also add enjoyable variety to your fishing.

Conclusions

When it comes to targeting trophy browns with dry flies, the size and shape of the flies trump characteristics such as color, wings, eyes, elaborate tails, etc. The brown trout fisherman should also spend more time reading and working productive water where it's obvious big browns are holding and less time changing patterns. A good cast of, at most, 35 to 40 feet in most situations, and one that is mended appropriately to compensate for currents, will take a lot more trout more often than longer efforts.

Also, I haven't made much of using tiny dries—#18 to 22—for a couple of reasons. While there are times when these work extremely well, especially when paired with 12- to 14-foot leaders tapered down to 6X or 7X (beyond this is a bit on the disingenuous side of deception), tying on, let alone seeing, these diminutive bits of fluff is difficult, and I prefer the not-difficult side of life. I've also found that larger patterns will take fish in many situations where browns are feeding on little bugs. The choice is yours, and I've included my favorite small fly pattern, a Blue-Winged Olive, below.

Finally, and chipping in from the well-informed esoteric realm of fly fishing that John Talia inhabits with righteous glee, my friend had this to say recently: "Browns love caddis, especially in the spring and fall! I once witnessed a 20-plus-incher literally come out of the water and beach himself, as he was convinced that catching one flying just above the surface was the only food that would satisfy him. Flopping/ sliding back into the water didn't seem to be much of a bother either based on the expression he had on his face. My theory on this is they love spicy! Although I have never tasted a caddis, a good friend of mine, David Decker, has and he says they are spicy. I once also witnessed a huge brown literally suspended under the surface film with his entire head to the end of his gill plate above the water line picking spring caddis out of the air on the Big Hole. Using his needle-nose beak, he would effectively pick at those spring caddis flying above the surface. Three of us tried to no avail drifting caddis to him for at least fifteen minutes. At times we would try to shoot the fly just above the surface, thinking our best chance was to hook him in the mouth as he fed 6 inches above the surface. The expression on this fish's face reminded me of the strange expressions I saw on the many faces of Deadheads at a Winterland concert in the mid-seventies. I think it confirms Decker's theory that they somehow get stoned on caddis . . . In the fall, swinging fall caddis nymphs through the tail-outs can result in vicious strikes—anything smaller than 3X tippet would be futile."

Elk Hair Caddis
Hook: TMC 900BL, sizes 10–20
Thread: To match body
Body: Antron or Haretron to match natural Hackle: Natural or dyed grizzly, palmered
Wing: Elk hair

Joe's Hopper
Hook: TMC 5212, sizes 6–14
Thread: Yellow
Tail: Red hackle fibers. Tie a loop of yellow poly yarn on top.
Body: Yellow poly yarn; alternatively, dubbing. Palmer with brown hackle, then trim the hackle close to the body on the sides.
Wing: Turkey wing quills. Treat with Flexament.
Hackle: Brown and grizzly, or Cree

Outlaw Hopper
Hook: Long dry fly, size 2X
Extended body: Gray yarn, twisted
Hackle: Furnace grade 3, palmered
Body: High-density gray foam
Head and collar: White deer hair

Yellow Humpy
Hook: TMC 100, sizes 10–18
Thread: Bright yellow or single strand of floss
Body: Bright yellow thread or floss
Tail: Light-colored elk
Wing: Elk or deer
Back: Light-colored elk
Note: This fly can be tied in a variety of colors.

Adams

Hook: TMC 100, sizes 10–20

Thread: 6/0 or 3/0, depending on size of hook

Tail: Moose hock

Wings: Grizzly hen hackle tips

Body: Gray beaver dubbing

Hackle: Brown and grizzly rooster

Blue-Winged Olive *(Baetis)*

Hook: Standard dry fly, sizes 14–24

Thread: Olive 8/0

Body: Olive dubbing

Tail: Dark blue dun hackle barbs

Hackle: Medium blue dun

Wing: Medium blue dun hen hackle tips

Rat-Faced McDougal

Hook: Standard dry fly, sizes 16–10

Thread: White 8/0 or 6/0. For the spun-hair body, gray size A rod-winding thread.

Tail: Ginger hackle fibers

Body: Spun and shaped deer or caribou hair

Wings: White calf tail

Hackle: Ginger

CHAPTER 4

Lurking Just Below the Surface

It has always been my private conviction that any man who pits
his intelligence against a fish and loses has it coming.

—John Steinbeck

Up until seventeen or eighteen years ago, I rarely fished just below
the surface. If I did, it was because a dry fly I was mismanaging
had succumbed to terminal drag and drowned. Emerger patterns, soft
hackles, caddis pupa—all of these were a mystery that held little attrac-
tion for me. Then one day I discovered a dozen Partridge and Orange
Soft Hackles in a plastic envelope in one of my tackle bags. I have no
idea how they got there. The capricious behavior of the angling deities
is most likely responsible. Armed with information I retained from a
fairly recent reading of Jock Scott's *Greased Line Fishing for Salmon*,
I decided to give them a try.

I wasn't expecting much as I began casting slightly upstream
along one of my favorite big brown trout runs. I figured I'd take a few
smaller fish of 12 to 14 inches and little else. Like it said in the book,
I maintained delicate contact with the fly, keeping the line just short
of being tight. About a dozen feet into the drift something tagged the
soft hackle, nearly jerking the rod from my right hand. No need to set

the hook—a large brown did the work for me as it thrashed, leaped, and tore up the surface of the, until then, quiet and deep run. I was using 3X tippet only because I was lackadaisical about the afternoon's fishing. This act of laziness prevented a break-off that would have certainly occurred if I'd tied on 18 inches of 5X like I should have done to match the #16 fly. The brown ran and jumped some more, making a tremendous splashy racket before calling it quits for the day. Looking at that fish was a revelation. I never imagined soft hackles or related patterns could provoke such a savage response from a trout of 5 pounds.

In the following weeks I acquired books by the soft-hackle guru, the late Sylvester Nemes—*The Soft-Hackled Fly* and *The Soft-Hackled Fly Addict*—and reread Scott's *Greased Line* and LaFontaine's *Trout Flies: Proven Patterns*. In the ensuing years I bought several more books on the subject by Nemes and Dave Hughes. What I learned has turned many an average day's fishing for smaller trout into excellent times spent connecting with and both landing and breaking off large trout. For a while I fished exclusively with soft hackles and LaFontaine's emerger patterns. But after several weeks I calmed down and incorporated this type of fishing into my repertoire of angling methods.

Emergers

The history of observing emerger insect activity goes back many years, as this relatively recent comment (1930) in *Taking Trout with the Dry Fly* by Samuel C. Camp demonstrates: "... for example, the more or less frequently occurring inability to induce a rise to the properly fished artificial, when its corresponding natural is hatching and 'apparent' rises to it are evidently numerous. It seems fair to assume that at such times the fish are feeding almost exclusively on the floating nymphs instead of the winged insects, taking the nymphs on the surface in practically the same way that the winged insect is taken, and quite possible in preference to the winged insect."

While Camp does not refer to emergers specifically, much of what he is seeing are clearly insects coming to and then breaking through a river's surface meniscus. Some years earlier, G. E. M Skues noticed the same thing on his beloved stretch of England's famed chalk stream, the Test. He spent much time and energy trying to convince his fellow fly fishers that their lack of success in taking big browns (a 4-pounder was and is a giant on the Test) was not from a lack of skill or casting expertise, but rather because they were misreading what was happening on the river. The rises they were casting dries to were not rises at all but rather the bulgings of the large fish as they arced just beneath the surface feeding on emergers, though again this term wasn't used.

I can't count the days that I futilely cast dry flies to large browns that were working steadily on what I thought were stoneflies, mayflies, or caddisflies lifting off into the wild blue yonder. Presentations I believed to be flawless were ignored by large trout with apparent disdain. The frustration as I ceaselessly changed patterns was unpleasant, making me anxious and unable, through my own self-absorption, to enjoy the day and surroundings. Reading LaFontaine's books and then having him give me a handful of his Sparkle Pupa emergers after a late afternoon's angling, while not changing my life, did dramatically improve my fishing on days when dry flies weren't the play. Gary's generosity (and there has never been a more giving man in fly fishing) opened a new realm of fishing for me. His book *Caddisflies* is not easy reading, not for the faint of heart, but it is a serious expansion on Schweibert's books, most notably *Nymphs*.

I hesitate to make a strong differentiation between soft hackles and emergers because I think that any distinction is small in scope and also not germane to the way I look at fly fishing. While switching from one to the other can mean the difference between some fish and some very big fish, observing the water and conditions to see what

> . . . observing the water and conditions to see what really is taking place is far more significant than incremental variations in pattern and technique.

really is taking place is far more significant than incremental variations in pattern and technique. I realize that many very good fly fishers will scoff at this and I will be pilloried at the very least. That's life.
Emerger fishing is more a refinement than a distinct field compared
to nymphing. Nymphs are more useful lower in the water column,
and they often require being tied weighted or with bead heads, or
weighted with varying sizes of split shot. Emergers work best as free-
floating patterns unencumbered by weight. Allowing them to weave
subtly through miniscule threads of current impart a lifelike action that
is most appealing to browns. Any addition of weight diminishes, if
not actually eliminates, this verisimilitude. One of the fascinations of
fly fishing is the opportunity to imitate life with such faithfulness that
an apex predator like a brown is fooled into taking a cleverly offered,
feathered deceit.

Emerger fly patterns are attempts to imitate aquatic insects—mainly
mayflies, caddisflies, and stoneflies—as they near the surface of a
river, creek, or lake, or when they first overcome the water's surface
tension. This stage of an insect's life is an important one for trout. The
bugs are concentrated in a narrow zone of the water column, often as
small as a few inches, and browns have an easier time feeding as the
insects move slowly to the surface. Once above the water the bugs
move with alacrity, as evidenced by the splashy, frenetic rises as fish
try to engulf the caddis, leaping to the air in an instant.

Emergers are a refinement on nymphs, bugs that work far
better lower in the water column, especially along the streambed.
LaFontaine's sparkle emergers use a tuft of Antron tied back over
the hook shank to mimic the air bubble that is normally attached to
pupae and nymphs as they reach the level of the water column just
below the surface and when pushing through the meniscus. Of all
the emerger patterns I've tried, those original designs by Gary work

Another good place to drift emergers, this small stream run has yielded browns over 2 pounds—trophy fish for this creek.

the best. He knew what he was doing. There were seasons when he spent more time observing the water than fishing. Also, I like his patterns because I really liked Gary. The key to fly fishing is a belief and confidence in your technique and ability to execute, the quality of the water, and the pattern itself.

The patterns are tied and fished unweighted. The only place I could see using weight would be in fast current, water I ignore with this method because the insects are not often present in good numbers. If I did fish this water, I would prefer using a short, low-density sink-tip line cast three-quarters upstream and worked several feet out from a bank or current seam, moving in a foot or so at a time. Most of the cast is a dead drift, though a slight mend imparting a motion toward the surface can be added if nothing happens along the drag-free way.

Working emergers involves the same casting angles as dry flies. Mends are steady throughout the drift in order to adjust to the constant changes in current speed and angles. When a sizable brown hits, the take is anything but delicate. The decision to feed is a dedicated one, and there is no hesitancy on the fish's part. For this reason I move up one size in tippet strength compared to similar nymph pattern sizes—5X to 4X, 6X to 5X, and so on.

One July afternoon with the sun cooking everything and the sky burning to a flat silver-white, the temperature around 100 degrees, I had one of those numerous mini-revelations that surface at odd moments in my day-to-day amblings. What at first appeared to be brown trout feeding on golden stone salmon flies rising from the surface were actually the bulging, subsurface takes of emergers by the trout.

I thought of what LaFontaine said about emergers being effective when dries aren't working, so I tied on an Emergent Sparkle Pupa. The first cast took a whitefish of 3 pounds. The next several casts did the same. Fun fishing, but I wanted some of the browns I could see bulging the river's surface about 40 to 50 feet away in water no more than 2 feet deep. I kept working the line in their direction, sifting through the eager whitefish, which I carefully released (after all, they're a native species). Finally I dropped the pattern about 3 feet in front of a nice fish who moved upstream to intercept the Sparkle Pupa with a classic surface bulge. I lifted the rod and the fish tore downstream across a shallow, gravel flat with its dorsal fin breaking the water. The brown had nowhere to go but managed to rile every fish within a large radius. Many of the other trout and the whitefish charged and circled the hooked brown, only to race away to deeper water. Finally I brought the fish to me and marked it on the rod. I was shocked at its size. The brown was close to 23 inches when I later measured the mark. Heft, maybe 4 pounds or more. After releasing the fish, I paused to let the feeding routine resume.

Good country here along the Marias, about forty-five minutes south of Chester. The river wanders through miles of fields, coulees, bluffs, and cliffs before emptying into the Tiber Reservoir, a massive impoundment covering nearly 15,000 acres. Billions of gallons of water lying out in the middle of intense aridness. Below Tiber Dam the water runs clear and cool, cold in spring and fall. While I said earlier I would not discuss tailwaters at length, this stretch of water is straightforward and uncrowded. The fishing exists, such as it is, because of the dam, and the river is not in the Bighorn, Beaverhead, Missouri class. Still, any trout out here in the freedom of the big open are an appreciated bonus.

In the spring large rainbows spawn in the clean gravels of the Marias, the well-oxygenated water providing perfect habitat for the incubating eggs and emerging fry. Come autumn, big browns move from their deepwater pocket pools downstream to run up into these gravels and build numerous redds.

For the big-fish trout hunter, these two times of the season are significant. Anyone willing to brave the often wickedly cold, brutal

This run on the Yellowstone is similar to the water mentioned that is related to the Marias, and produces large browns on emergers.

winds that drive glass-like sleet and snow into the skin, anyone willing to cast weighted streamers like Marabou Muddlers and Woolly Buggers into the teeth of a gale, has a legitimate opportunity to connect with a rainbow or brown of several pounds. The fish are aggressive at these times of breeding and fight like hell. I used to come here for this fishing on a regular basis years ago, but have pretty much given up on chasing trout during spawning time. The fish have enough troubles trying to reproduce, let alone survive, without my crazed efforts. Biologists have told me that hooking the fish, playing them quickly, and carefully releasing them ensures their survival, which is good. The fishing for the 3 or so miles below the dam is excellent and worthwhile.

I returned to casting for big browns. There seemed to be at least a dozen working in small pods upstream. I shot another cast ahead of a fish feeding close by, and it eagerly took the emerger. Not as big as the first, but 3 pounds. The next two hours were more of the same: spotting individual browns, then casting and often sifting through the whitefish and a couple nice rainbows of 16 inches, and then the browns. All of them were over 2 pounds and up to 4-plus. Observing closely what was going on—not dry fly action, but rather just-below-the-surface emerger action—and using Gary's pattern produced a wonderful afternoon filled with big browns.

I've experienced similar situations on the upper Clark Fork not far from Warm Springs below the Hog Holes. Lots of dry flies but no trout, then a shift to an Emergent Sparkle Pupa pattern and, like a switch being flipped, brown after brown and all of them 18 inches and larger. I've also had analogous results on the Teton below Choteau and on the Dearborn and the Jefferson.

Soft Hackles

Remembering that 90 percent or more of a trout's diet (especially trophy browns) consists of food taken below the surface should influence serious big-trout seekers as to both pattern and technique. While big browns are ardent cannibals, there are also many times when they feed on aquatic insects nearing the surface. Emergers, as already discussed, are very good at taking large trout in the right setting. The same is true of soft hackles, which have been catching fish for centuries, as Sylvester Nemes writes in the introduction to his book *Two Centuries of Soft-Hackled Flies:* "The history starts with Richard's Bowlker's *Art of Angling*, published in 1747. He must have done a good job with that book, because his son, Charles, continued to publish it for many years into the nineteenth century . . . Nowadays we have weighted bead-heads, which cannot be called flies and are better suited with a spinning rod than a fly rod. Some anglers and guides tie droppers up on their leaders, thereby creating some of the most efficient snagging machines ever used by fly fishers. I feel that this book shows that soft-hackle flies play a far greater role in fly fishing than anyone might have imagined."

Nemes passed away in 2010, but his legacy lives on. I agree with everything he said above. Since I began using soft hackles, I've taken many more and larger fish over the course of a season than I had in the past. His patterns and approaches filled a hole in my angling bag of tactics. And his disgust with bead heads and droppers mirrors my own. I realize that I'm dancing with my own brand of hypocrisy since I use split shot, mainly for Woolly Buggers and larger nymphs, but there's just something about bead heads that bothers me. Someday I'll define my aversion, maybe. His stating this position propelled me to return to fishing without droppers, and relying less on strike indicators as well. Less is more in so many aspects of life.

When I first started using soft hackles, I had a hard time believing that any fly that was tied so sparsely would catch fish. But then I recalled the Biggs' Special I use on lakes and slower portions of rivers. This fly is basically a little bit of nothing, but it works really well. Whenever I tied it thicker, perhaps thinking of Woolly Buggers,

A nice brown took a soft-hackle pattern one hot July afternoon. Notice the
shallow water shelving into a relatively deep run. The take was several feet into
this water.

the success rate plummeted. With soft hackles, the few barbules of hackle impart a realism that denser ties do not.

Of all of the soft hackles, the Partridge and Orange is my favorite. This one outperforms all others for me, including variations of green, olive, yellow, and red along with distinctly different soft-hackle patterns. To be honest, I believe that this is largely a function of my faith in the pattern. Given only a March Brown or Hare's Ear soft hackle, I have a suspicion that each would do as well as my favorite if it were fished as often, thoroughly, and with the same amount of faith in their success.

A mistake I made early on was casting three-quarters upstream, or even directly upstream, allowing the soft hackle to drop down below its effective range in the water column. Jock Scott wrote decades ago that the ideal presentation is just slightly upstream, or even directly across stream, with sufficient length to cover a targeted fish (in his case, Atlantic salmon) for only a select few feet of drift. He eschewed allowing the fly to swing out at the end on all but a very few occasions. On this I disagree, having taken many browns on the tail end of a drift, the fish tearing into the slightly dressed fly. The swing of the line and leader in the current impart an action to a soft hackle that some trout find hard to resist, much like an Elk Hair doing the same dance, only on the surface. This might be only a function of individual preference. Some people like Scotch, others prefer Bourbon.

Similar to emergers, soft hackles imitate insects as they near or contact the surface. With this in mind, the fly should remain in the first several inches of water below the surface. The angler should maintain contact with the fly but not straighten the line, instead allowing only the slightest suppleness or slack that will in turn allow a lifelike float and movement. Very slight mends are often needed to achieve this. As a result, a cast of more than 40 feet is a long cast when working soft hackles. Even on large western rivers, casts over 40 feet are often counterproductive. Cut the river down to size and fish the

This brown took a soft hackle on a small, central Montana stream in late August,
a time when fishing is normally very slow.

On moving water, 40 feet is plenty of distance if the approach is stealthy and the cast is relatively discreet.

now-manageable stretches as you would a smaller river. I love watching the artistes drifting by me when I'm enjoying the Yellowstone from shore. They're launching 90-foot casts with such windblown elegance while the guides look down at the water sloshing around in the boat, the poor guys having given up on rowing closer to the bank in a vain attempt at gently showing their sports that line control, fly control, any control is needed. On moving water, 40 feet is plenty of distance if the approach is stealthy and the cast is relatively discreet. Longer efforts often smack of double-haul ostentation.

Fishing soft hackles, the leaders should be more than 7 feet long but not much beyond 9, and taper to 4X, maybe less. The 4X size is the one I use most frequently not only for soft hackles, but also for most other types of flies. TroutHunter offers leaders of 8 feet in 4.5X that are ideal for this type of action. When the standard drag-free drift fails to produce, slight, 2- or 3-inch strips of line to mimic the motion of an insect making its way toward the surface might do the trick.

Soft hackles and their contemporaries, emerger patterns, cover the first foot or so of a river's water column, an area that receives less attention than it should. Large browns cruise this water, feeding eagerly on caddisflies, mayflies, and stoneflies as they move into a river's subsurface environment. When fish appear to be rising but refuse dry flies, switch to emergers or soft hackles. That's all there is to this. Nothing more, nothing less.

LaFontaine's Emergent Sparkle Pupa

Hook: Tiemco 3769, sizes 10–18, or other 2X heavy nymph hook

Thread: Brown 6/0 UNI-Thread

Head: Tan or beige Antron dubbing

Wing: Elk hair

Pupa case: Amber Antron

Body: Amber Antron

Tail: Clear or white Antron yarn

Partridge and Orange Soft Hackle

Hook: Wet fly, sizes 12–16

Thread: Orange 6/0, or Pearsall's orange tying silk

Body: Orange floss, or Pearsall's orange tying silk (red, green, or other colors may be substituted)

Hackle: Gray partridge, about 2 turns

CHAPTER 5

Subterranean Excursions

I love fishing. You put that line in the water and you don't know what's on the other end. Your imagination is under there.

—Robert Altman

The run along the grassy bank was classic big fish water. This was always a place for hopper patterns on hot, breezy days or, when the weather turned overcast, a #6 Woolly Bugger cast tight to the bank and then stripped erratically back home. There were browns here. Big ones. I'd taken them over 2 feet and 4 or more pounds. They were the kind of browns that are dark colored with pronounced kypes and lots of wicked teeth. Browns at their best in fighting trim.

I decided for some reason to tie on my rendition of Charles Brooks's legendary, if not infamous, nymph creation, the Assam Dragon. This is a big, furry, ugly thing that looks like a distant relative of the Woolly Bugger, an individual descended from a family that probably spent way too much time in close proximity to each other back in some timbered hollow that was the scene for a SyFy Channel Grade Z horror flick, along the lines of *Wrong Turn 2: Dead End.* (I am an aficionado of art films. Who can ever forget *I Spit on Your Grave?*) The one I'd attached to a 8-foot leader tapered to 3X was weighted

Plopping a weighted nymph tight to a grassy, undercut bank—a perfect big brown holding spot.

on a long-shank #6—a really delicate example of the fly tier's and fly fisher's art.

Where the current curled slightly around a protrusion in the bank, an eddy marked by a light covering of root beer–colored foam, I dropped the Assam with the delicacy of a bar of soap slipping from my hand during a shower. I made sure to work out a little more line than needed to cover the 30 feet from me to the bank. I lightly checked the cast right at the end of the forward stroke, causing the fly to drop straight down inches from the bank. The line curved a touch downstream with enough slack to allow the nymph to sink quickly toward the streambed where I knew big browns like to hold. Once the Assam was where I wanted it to be (or at least where I imagined it to be), I lightly pulled in sufficient line so that my contact with the fly was tight but not taut.

Three feet of drift later, my decision to try a new approach on this run was rewarded when I saw the spot where the leader and fly line joined stop abruptly in its downriver movement. I reached back briskly and instantly felt the weight of a heavy fish. I jerked the rod back three times to make sure the hook was firmly set. The action triggered an angry reaction. A male brown (the kype was distinct) of several pounds leaped above the surface, crashed back down, and repeated the effort before running 100 feet downstream to sound in a deep pool. The sound of the 1946 Thompson 100 was wonderful as line whizzed off it, and the Edwards Special was bowed in a classic curve heralding a firm connection with a sizable trout. The brown sulked as I splashed rapidly down to a gravel bank above the fish, frantically reeling in slack as I went.

Putting pressure on the fish only transmitted a steady thrumming up the line to my grip on the rod. The stalemate lasted a minute. My next pull brought the brown flying up from the depths, where it thrashed much of the pool's calm surface into a series of concentric circles that washed into each other. Above me at the head of the pool I caught the silvery flickers of a herd of whitefish fleeing for the calm and safety upriver. A strong jerk on the line refocused my attention on the brown. The fish powered back and forth, tried to dive again, but tired against the flexible force of the rod. When it came to my feet, I dropped to my knees that made audible cracking sounds, reminding me that I wasn't in the land of youth anymore.

I admired the brown, glowing with the intense colors of approaching spawning. The fish stared at me. No, that's not right. This brown's gaze, as I twisted the point free with thumb and forefinger, bored through me like that of a bad-ass judge about to pass sentence on

This brown came as the result of bank-tight casting of a large nymph.

a child support scofflaw. The last turn of the hook gave the male an opportunity to take a swipe at my hand. Razor-sharp teeth drew blood on my knuckle and the soft tissue between my fingers. The brown held still for a moment, then slowly cruised away from me, soon out of sight in dark water.

I watched the blood drip from my hand into shallow water. Tiny minnows raced through the small clouds of red as though they were feeding on me. I'd caught a 4- or 5-pound fish on an Assam Dragon, something I'd never tried here before over the years, but I wondered, "Who won this encounter?"

Nymphing Odds and Ends

A few days on the water gaining experience quickly leads to nymphing success. Like anything new, the various and often numerous things involved with taking large browns with nymphs can seem daunting to the neophyte and even at times to someone who's fished beneath the surface a great deal.

I try not to cast more than 35 feet, and in fast water flowing around rocks or logjams, my approach is more that of dappling with a dry fly. I extend arm and rod out to a likely holding area and run the nymph through the hole, following nearly directly above it with the rod tip. In most situations the 35-foot-cast rule is invoked either quartering upstream along undercut banks or weed bed edges, or in the center of slowly revolving eddies. I find that any more line out, while possibly reaching a trout tucked tight to a distant bank, causes too much play in the line for a decent presentation or a solid set of the hook. Allow the nymph to sink for several seconds, maybe as many as ten, before initiating a series of short lift-retrieves of 2 to 3 inches at a medium pace. This is faster than the natural but tends to attract attention without scaring off any feeding trout. Then let the pattern fall back down toward the streambed before repeating the process. If this is the appropriate technique for the time and conditions, the browns will take within seconds of the end of the lift. The pattern will rarely reach the bottom of the stream.

When using nymphs I rarely use a leader of more than 7 feet. In heavy water I'll sometimes work with 5 feet, 2X or larger its entire length. Delicacy with big nymphs hasn't proven to be of high necessity when it comes to large trout. And I prefer nylon leaders and tippet. Fluorocarbon seems a bit stiff. A friend of mine and longtime angling companion Jake Howe said, "I don't use fluorocarbon. There's very little give, and when it says, say, 4-pound test, that's it. I've checked and that's what it will always break at." This is a matter of preference. I know others who swear by the newer fiber.

Sometimes conditions require changing lines; for example, from a weight-forward 5-weight to a 4-foot sink tip in the same weight. I used to change spools, but now I change reels. It is just as easy and only marginally heavier to carry an extra reel as opposed to an additional spool. I rarely bring along either, figuring along the hackneyed line of "I'll dance with the one that brung me." Unless the stretch of river I'm planning to fish has a truly wide degree of conditions, one line suffices. Perhaps all this is nothing more than specious behavior on my part, but every action that takes time from a pattern being on or beneath the water is time when a brown won't be able to take my fly.

The use of nymphs goes back centuries and, for almost as many years, has sometimes been looked down upon by dry fly purists as a crude, unethical way to take trout. That's the purists' problem. Matters of tactical finesses and discretion have no place in the examination of what is needed to catch large brown trout.

Droppers, Indicators, and Other Gear

In a recent conversation with Livingston guide, home remodeler, and friend Dan Lahren, he offered this concerning nymph fishing: "Rarely, due to fishing pressure, does one find a sizable brown trout that eats smaller dry flies, with the exception of a stonefly or a grasshopper

Nymping shallow runs that give way to pools and sheltered banks nearly always turn large trout.

imitation. At a certain age they shift from small insects to fish, mice, and the large insects. Shooting heads with streamers or large nymphs in the spring and fall seem to be the most productive way of catching large brown trout." Ugly rumor has it that Lahren regularly guides writers Jim Harrison and Carl Hiaasen down the Yellowstone. "There is a three-week window as the water is clearing from runoff on the western rivers that one can catch large fish from a boat casting to shore and stripping or dead-drifting streamers and big nymphs," Lahren continued. "And mid to late summer the 'bobber and nymph' works, where one puts on a balloon or one of the many other brightly colored floating devices above nymphs and streamers. This technique I detest, as I see the bobber in my dreams and my dream life is all I have."

I'm no fan of droppers. The rigs tend to complicate the fishing. I'm always untangling the tippets, and I've had too many foul hooks from a trout taking the dropper, arcing over and back down through the water column, and then snagging himself on the dry fly. I realize that the classic wet fly practitioners often used three patterns at once. Good for them. Once again, I'll shun the practice. One fly is plenty. In fact, working one fly thoroughly and correctly is more effective far more often than all of the high-tech, sophisticated messes mentioned above. Disagree at your pleasure. While you're stringing together various tippets, flies, and knots, I'll be working over browns.

I'm not against indicators with the vehemence of Lahren. I mostly agree with his view on the matter, especially the "bobber" reference, but there are times when indicators make things easier and more efficient. When the current is fast and deep, an indicator helps control the depth that a nymph travels through the water. In low-light conditions an indicator is the difference between late and missed takes and hooking fish. I prefer orange to other colors for the visibility factor. The browns don't care if it's green, white, or pink.

I always use either barbless hooks or hooks with the barbs pinched down, as much for the ease of release as anything. Ease translating to less bloodshed both from the trout and my hands.

One last point that has nothing to do with catching trout: When changing tippet or taking off an indicator, stuff the used tackle in a pocket. Discarded line and indicators along banks look like hell, but worse, birds and small mammals have died choking to death or strangling their intestines in line. Also, when I use split shot, I use steel and not lead. Lead works better, but steel is less intrusive on the environment. I feel the same way about stream cleats. Sure, they work great on slippery surfaces, but the scarring of rocks and gravel can be devastating to spawning substrate, and there's nothing more exciting when fly fishing a favorite stretch than following a trail of rock and stone scrubbed bare by metal cleats. Montana's concern with felt soles transmitting whirling disease is well intentioned, but it smacks of "Elvis has left the building." Cleaning waders, boots, sandals, and other gear is far more useful than changing from felt to cleats or hard rubber, which is a bit like walking on a surface of graphite-coated ball bearings. One biologist told me that he's convinced that birds and mammals like herons, hawks, kingfishers, martens, and beavers transfer diseases at a far greater rate than humans, most frequently via excrement and urine. The choice is yours on this. I prefer taking the time to clean my equipment to scouring streambeds.

Spring's High Waters Are Also Opportunities

From mid-March through early May, water levels in my part of Montana are low, sometimes resembling midsummer flows. But within days these streams can rise and go off-color from a combination of snowmelt and spring rain. This usually spells the end of fishing until late June at the earliest, though some of the better-behaved waters provide fishing that often turns large browns and other trout. As an example, during the recent salmon fly hatch on the Yellowstone, the water was turbid, high, and cold. Out of frustration, I dropped an Assam Dragon, an ugly-looking thing designed by Charles Brooks, into a swirling eddy next to shore. Three straight casts letting the #4 nymph sink and spin in the brown water produced three fish, all of them 18 inches or larger, all browns, and all within fifteen minutes. Not the most challenging or aesthetic angling, but very rewarding. At other spots of similar dimensions on rivers that include the Marias, Bitterroot, Flathead, and Smith, I've experienced similar results using Woolly Buggers, sculpin ties, and the Assam Dragon. The fish are mostly large and mostly browns. There have been instances of futility, but they have been uncommon.

This being said, high water is tough to work most of the time. The fly must get down to the slower water along the streambed, where calm currents allow browns a place of shelter. I've seen this referred to as a benthic zone, but this is a term more accurately applied to lakes, ponds, and oceans. The calmer currents in streams are caused by the friction of water moving across cobble, gravel, and stones, and related hydraulics.

So where are the big browns when the water is off-color and high?

"Look for fish in a location where the water's velocity isn't so great," former Montana Department of Fish, Wildlife & Parks fisheries biologist Joe Houston told me some years ago in answer to my frustration. "Fish all the holes and pocket water with streamers, wet flies, and nymphs, right on the bottom. In roily water, stay away from the middle and upper strata—the high-velocity water."

Houston went on to say that turbidity has little effect on trout, something I'd been unaware of, but a fish has to eat regardless of conditions. They usually stay put if they can find a quiet place. The one notable exception, according to Houston, is the whitefish, which move out of muddy water and into clear feeder streams. The fish will be sluggish in this colder water, so patience and thoroughness is a virtue.

Even though the water is high and off-color during spring runoff, there are still
fish to be had in relatively calm, sheltered spots like this one.

If there are fish holding in the clouded flow, sometimes a dozen or more casts are needed. One way to get a streamer or large nymph down to the browns in deepwater holes is by using the Brooks Method invented by the late Charles Brooks of West Yellowstone. Brooks consistently caught large trout over 5 pounds with his technique. It's hard to master but, once learned, is efficient, less tiring, and consistently effective. In distillate form, the Brooks Method is as follows:

Use a leader from 4 to 6 feet long with a tip of 0.010 to 0.012 inches in diameter. Tippet strength is needed to hold big fish in big water. Leader shyness is not an issue. A moderately stiff, 8'6" rod handles the work. Depending on depth, a sink-tip line of at least 5 feet makes a big difference, though added weight at the head of a pattern works, too, especially in combination with a sink tip. Casting all of this requires practice, patience, and on occasion a high pain threshold. All of my large nymphs and streamers are tied with wire up to 0.030, which further helps to reach the bottom of a river.

I don't use strike indicators all that often, usually when the water is high and flowing quite fast. I prefer sensing the strike through a combination of line movements and acquired intuition. Indicators disrupt the movement, in my eyes. When starting out with this style of fishing, however, strike indicators are a good way to both learn when a fish is taking and follow the drift path of the fly. As experience is acquired, eliminating the indicator allows for a more natural float most of the time.

Establish a position about 20 feet upstream and 5 feet from the edge of the run to be fished. The first cast should be about 15 feet upstream and 6 feet out. Allow the pattern to dredge the bottom while you still control slack and maintain gentle contact. This is a matter of feel, experience, and practice. The line should not be taut nor should it have slack and belly in the current. Just short of taut is the ideal, and often involves a steady series of slight mid-line mends both up- and

> If there are fish holding in the clouded flow, sometimes a dozen or more casts are needed.

downstream. A small flick of the wrist on the rod hand while lifting the rod a few inches does the trick.

To quote Charles Brooks in his book *Nymph Fishing for Larger Trout,* "As the fly and line move downstream, the rod tip is lifted so that only a slight droop is in the line between the rod tip and the water."

The angler pivots with the line, keeping the "slight droop" in order to keep the fly working along the bottom as long as possible. Too tight a line and the fly lifts. Too much slack and strikes are missed. At the end of the drift, wait several seconds, allowing any bow in the line to straighten and the pattern to waver in the rushing water. I strike by holding the line and raising the rod tip. I used to also strike simultaneously with the rod lift by stripping line, but have found this to be unnecessary and to lead to increased break-offs.

The pickup and subsequent upstream cast (one motion) is the most difficult part of the method. Raise the rod parallel to the water until it's shoulder high, extending the line hand toward the stripping guide. Then strip down toward the hip with the line hand while backhanding the rod upstream, an action that Brooks says is similar to a "tennis backhand." Stop the cast just as the rod tip points slightly upstream across from you. If the cast is less than successful, a quick downstream roll cast and quicker pickup will put the line and fly back in play.

After five or six casts, strip off several feet of line and repeat the process. Strip off line in 3- to 4-foot increments until 35 to 40 feet of line is out. Then move upstream a dozen feet or so and begin again. All of this can become tedious when no browns are taken or are few in number. Still, in my mind, any casting beats sitting at home watching ESPN.

In Karel Krivanec's *Czech Nymph and Other Related Fly Fishing Methods,* this method is refined to the point where the angler is fishing straight-line leaders of only a few feet. This was devised for fast, clear water but has worked for me in high, muddy conditions. The only problem is that the takes are so abrupt and fierce that the leader often snaps and there is an ever-present threat of rod tips snapping in the gay spring winds.

A Little Damselfly Music

Understanding anything in life more often than not comes about through a harmonious collision between luck and exasperated experimentation. This is the case with damselfly nymphs and my hit-or-miss learning curve. Fortunately, in this instance, fate and persistence mixed to make the heady cocktail while adding a slight increase to my fish-taking skills.

Working damselfly *(Odanata)* nymphs along quiet stretches of streams, barely moving eddies, and backwaters—especially on the edges of weed beds and during hot late spring and summer days— will take large browns when other methods prove futile. The creatures have turned lifeless dog days of summer outings into something more entertaining.

One July afternoon on a pond-like stretch of the Marias, I decided to use a nymph known as the Biggs' Special, or Sheep Creek Special. The decision came out of both desperation and curiosity. The place was several miles below Tiber Dam. I'd noticed a number of the electric blue damsels buzzing over the river's surface, so I tied on the Biggs' Special, a pattern that imitates the nymph of this and other lake insects. The fly was weighted with 0.020 wire, so it sank below the surface with little trouble. I followed the drift and used a slight lift, as in the Leisenring Lift described by James Leisenring more than seventy years ago. I wrote about this method in an article for *Fly Fisherman Magazine* in 1985, but rarely take advantage of the technique. The first cast turned a brown of 18 inches, and subsequent efforts took fish up to 22 inches, the largest 4 pounds. The method is simple: Cast quartering upstream, allowing the pattern to sink, and then strip a few

Calm, smooth stretches such as these often hold damselfly and dragonfly nymphs during summer months.

inches of line to mimic the nymph as it struggles to reach the surface and become airborne. All of the takes, most of them fierce strikes, came within seconds of ending the lift when the fly was motionless or just beginning to drop back down through the water column. I started with 4X but soon went up to 3x to avoid the break-offs caused by the aggressiveness of the browns.

Years ago Montana Department of Fish, Wildlife & Parks biologist Tom Weaver shared information with me about trout and damselflies: "Fish root for them along the bottom early in the year, but as the water warms they begin looking for the nymphs closer to the surface. To some extent, they are keyed into them all of the time, even in slow-moving water."

The majority of the damselfly's life is spent in a series of naiadal, or nymphal, stages. And because they are present and moving about much of the year, browns have learned to feed on them. The nymphs bear little resemblance to the streamlined damselflies, and actually don't look much like the Biggs' Special—the pattern is slim, where the nymphs are bulkier. Perhaps the slight hackle creates the illusion of reality. The stout, chunky nymph is usually gray-olive, and subdued in color. The body may be smooth or rough with small spines, and is often covered with a growth of filamentous algae or stream detritus. The naiads are often found on submerged vegetation along the bottoms of lakes, ponds, reservoirs, and stillwater areas of rivers and creeks. A one-year life cycle is the norm, though there is substantial variation among species. There is often more than one generation per year, but at the other end of the spectrum, some members may require more than four years to complete a life cycle. Much of this time is spent crawling along the bottom of its natal waters and along aquatic plant stems and leaves.

Odonata nymphs may be roughly classified as either climbers, sprawlers, or burrowers. The first two types attract the most attention from trout. Most of the sprawlers have long legs and are slow-moving, dull-colored animals that occur on a variety of types of subsurface environments. Damselfly nymphs are most vulnerable at two times in their lives—when feeding or rising to the surface to hatch. The latter is the most important for fly fishers.

Although all *Odonata* nymphs are carnivorous, the methods of feeding vary. Some species carefully stalk their prey. Many of the burrowing forms remain motionless, with only the pulsating motion of their gills indicating life, as they wait for food to move within striking distance. They may remain in this state for days at a time before moving with lightning-like quickness to pounce on a food source. This lack of movement explains why this form of damselfly is low on the trout's food list, and as a result, the angler's list as well. The very large nymphs can seize prey up to an inch away through a combination of labium (the liplike structure of the nymph) action and a quick, forward-lurching movement.

"Once trout key into them, they really feed on them to the exclusion of almost anything else," said biologist Weaver. "And this action increases as the water temperature increases."

The fact that damselfly nymphs are large and easy to spot makes them attractive targets for browns, far more so than the adults that zip and zing above the surface. Patterns imitating the adult form are pleasing to the angler's eye, but not in the same league as the Biggs' Special in terms of catching fish.

> The fact that damselfly nymphs are large and easy to spot makes them attractive targets for browns . . .

Most *Odonata* emerge in the morning or late afternoon, with very few making the move during midday or in darkness. "The pre-hatch ritual often includes distinct swimming movements that consist of two, three, or four trips from the bottom to the surface and back down again before they are able to break the surface film and get into the air to dry off," said Weaver. "This is a perilous existence, and the trout really hammer them at this time."

The dropping back to the bottom explains the hard takes at the conclusion of the lift of the fly, and that brief period before it begins to gain speed as it sinks down through the water. Imitating this motion is not difficult, mainly a brief, gentle left and then letting the pattern fall on its own. Nine-foot leaders of 3X work best. Smaller leads to break-offs, while stouter hinders the lifelike motion and is also more visible to the trout in still water.

A Most Curious Approach

I was first shown this unusual nymphing method while fishing for rainbows on the lakes of the Blackfeet Reservation with Joe Kipp. Since then I've used the identical procedure on rivers in late winter and early spring when moving water is carving out openings in the ice. The cover provided by the thinning ice shelves holds trout, sometimes very big browns that will take a nymph if it is fished as described here . . .

The edge of the retreating ice was about 50 feet from the shore. As the stuff melted and broke up, we could hear large booms and a sound like a train makes when it pulls the slack out of a mile of freight cars and the couplings slam together. Chief Mountain was a black monolith outlined by the setting sun. The ice-free water in front of us was so clear, we could see cruising fish 20 feet down.

"Watch this, John!" Kipp yelled as he waded out into the frigid water. The air temp was in the 50s but the water was near freezing. We were wearing thick neoprene waders, long underwear, sweaters, and fingerless mittens. Late April is a time of warmth and magnolia blossoms down south. Up here on the northern high plains, the climate is a mixture of winter that refuses to leave and the joy of warm weather. Kipp worked his line out over the ice and landed a Hare's Ear Nymph several feet on the ice. He then began inching it toward the water in sporadic, quick jerks. What the hell was he doing? I'd only met him yesterday and up to this point he seemed like a likeable, reasonably sane, happy guy.

"We call this ice fishing, John," and his laughter mixed with the crackling ice and tinkling ice crystals.

I looked on as he pulled the fly right to the edge and then jerked it into the water. The moment the nymph touched the surface a submarine shape raced out and, in a boiling swirl of red, green, and chrome, nailed the fly. Kipp set the hook and the rainbow tore back underneath the ice.

"He's tail-walking now, John," Kipp said (he's always used my name with great frequency). "Upside down on the bottom of the ice," and more laughter flew across the ice. Eventually he brought the fish to shore, and I was there to admire it. Nearly 2 feet of pure, hard, colorful muscle.

"A small one, John. Maybe 6 pounds," and he turned it loose. "We'll catch bigger ones at a lake I'm taking you to tomorrow, and the really big fish will be out when you come back in May."

I tried my hand at this "ice fishing" and took a couple of rainbows of around 3 pounds. Joe pronounced my efforts as "Not bad, John."

Since that day I've experimented on rivers from the North Fork of the Flathead to the Sun to the Clarks Fork of the Yellowstone. I've always taken fish. The largest was a 26- to 27-inch brown on the Yellowstone a few miles below Reed Point. You'll never have twenty- or thirty-fish days doing this, but the fish you catch will be a surprise as they zip out from beneath the ice, grab the nymph as it hits the water, and then rush back for cover. One of my favorite patterns is the Fledermaus. It has the size and the bugginess to work well in heavy water if trout don't take when it slides off the ice and into the river. Its size also helps to create a racket as the fly is dragged across the frozen water surrounding the open channel. And using this bug, my average fish size is always larger than I normally take from a given stretch. Maybe it will work for you. Nothing to lose by trying.

The following few knots handle all of my needs, not just nymphs. While many fly fishers are superb knot tiers. I'm not one of them. I

Big bugs once flew here, as this salmon fly husk indicates. Large nymphs or even a dead-drifted Bugger might still work.

depend on very few knots. Among them are the improved clinch for tying flies to leader and, on rare occasions, the Turle for nymphs; the nail knot for splicing backing to fly line and leader butt to fly line; the surgeon's knot for adding tippet; the surgeon's loop for all sorts of needs; the dropper loop for those rare, and I mean rare, times when I use a dropper and risk the madness that goes with tangles; and the arbor knot for attaching backing to a reel.

Sometimes I change from a floating line to a sink tip or shooting head. Instead of spare spools, I carry another reel or two. This forces me to retreat to the bank, eliminating the loss of fumbled spools in the river. Eliminating mistakes in all aspects of life is important.

Assam Dragon

Hook: Size 4 or 2X long

Weight: 0.030 non-lead wire, 12 wraps

Body: Natural brown fur similar to seal skin, ⅛ inch wide and 3–4 inches long

Hackle: Brown dyed grizzly, long and soft. Tie in hackle by the butt with the wrong side toward the eye of the hook.

Thread: Brown 3/0 nylon

Biggs' Special, aka Sheep Creek Special

Hook: TMC 5262, sizes 8–16

Thread: Dark olive

Tail: Brown hackle wound on the shank, as for a dry fly

Body: Dark olive chenille

Wing: 5–7 mallard flank fibers

Hare's Ear Nymph
Hook: TMC 3769 or equivalent, sizes 8–18
Thread: Camel 8/0 UNI-Thread
Tail: Guard hairs from hare's mask, tied short
Rib: Lagartun gold oval tinsel, fine or small, depending on size. Some tiers also use Mylar.
Abdomen: Hare's mask with guard hairs (longer, more developed hair)
Lead: 0.025–0.010
Wing case: Turkey tail or wing, width equal to the gap of hook
Thorax: Hare's mask with guard hairs

Pheasant Tail Nymph
Hook: Wet fly or nymph, sizes 8–20
Thread: Black or brown 8/0
Tail: Pheasant tail (male)
Rib: Copper wire
Body: Pheasant
Wing case: Pheasant
Thorax: Hare's ear
Legs: Pheasant

Squirrel Tail Nymph
Hook: TMC 5263, sizes 6–12
Thread: Black
Tail: Hare's mask
Rib: Gold tinsel
Body: Red fox squirrel mixed with brown and black Antron
Legs: Mottled brown hen hackle

Fledermaus, by Jack Schneider
Hook: Mustad 3906B or equivalent, sizes 4–16
Thread: Black 3/0
Body: Dubbed full from muskrat fur
Wing: Gray squirrel tail hairs, extending above bend

A brown fearlessly will look you straight in the eye as if to say "This isn't over yet."

CHAPTER 6

That Old Ace in the Hole

Fishing tournaments seem a little like playing tennis with living balls...

—Jim Harrison, *Just Before Dark*, 1991

Cobble streambed, millions of gallons of springwater perking up, thick aquatic vegetation, lush backside growth, caddisflies, mayflies, hoppers, sculpins, damselflies, rainbow trout, and lots of browns, some of them large and ill-tempered. "Time for some big trout," I said to Ginny as I rigged up a 5-weight with a brown Woolly Bugger and a couple of split shot. "Bring your camera along and let's go."

I worked every tiny pocket or undercut, each pool and run, the Bugger banging off brush or slamming into the water. Smaller browns fled for shelter under the onslaught. Eventually I made a cast that seemed to snag on the bottom. I pulled back on the rod. Nothing. Bottom. A log. Then the line ripped upstream, downstream, under the bank, and back out in the middle of the pool.

A brown and a nice one. The unruly creature held on the bottom and shook his head. Several runs and head thrashings later, I drug the brown into the shallow water at my feet. Eighteen inches, fat, deep brown, copper, and gold with large black spots, and tiny gold flaking along the shoulders. A beautiful trout. One of the best. Hell, they all are. Lots of rapid photos, a release, and the brown buried its head in the weeds at Ginny's feet. He sulked for several minutes before she nudged its back, and it streaked for the dark shelter of the far bank.

"That's all I wanted. What I was after," I said. "I know how to bugger." One lousy brown and I was the world's best. I know better, but one wild fish destroys any sense of reason or humility I may possess. We walked back to camp happy and relaxed.

Anyone who knows me even a little bit where fly fishing is concerned is aware of the fact that I love to fish Woolly Buggers, particularly a Cree-hackled item of my own ratty design parameters. I've taken more browns over 20 inches—and rainbows, brookies, cutthroats, bull trout, arctic char, northerns, and smallmouth bass—on this pattern than all the others I use combined. To be fair, aside from the pattern's effectiveness and my ability to use it, one of the other main reasons is that when in doubt about a new water or what trout are taking on home waters, I tie on the Cree-hackled Bugger. While I've listed, at the end of this chapter, a few other streamer patterns I like, the Bugger is my favorite, and once the techniques are learned, they apply to the other streamer patterns as well.

I first started using Buggers with enthusiasm more than twenty years ago on the Bitterroot. One October, John Talia showed me how truly wicked they could be in taking large brown trout. Back in those days we had the river pretty much to ourselves. Anyone else we ran into, and this was one or two other outfits at the most, were known to John. We'd all say "Hello," talk about the fishing, the weather, the baseball playoffs, then go our merry ways. As we neared the takeout by the lodge he used to own, John pulled over along a wide gravel bar below an enormous emerald pool that must have been well over a dozen feet deep in places. He tied on a large black Bugger that he said was heavily weighted with wire, and cast out 50 feet of line before

Woolly Buggers have resulted in more trophy browns for me than any other pattern.

aiming a cast far up the pool along the inside bank. He allowed the pattern to sink, roll, and twist its way to the bottom without taking in much line. The Bugger worked around in the eddy for a long time—not a full minute but close to it—before John stripped in most of the slack and started to impart life to the imitation with quick strips of line. About the third pull resulted in a powerful tug in the opposite direction. John lifted his rod to set the hook, and seconds later an enormous brown blasted through the surface before running and leaping across the pool, east to west and north to south. After a couple of minutes, the fish was brought to the shallows near shore.

"Hell of a brown, Talia," I said. "What do you think? Twenty-six inches?"

"No way, Holt. I'd say 23 or 24, but the thing is a boxcar," he said and laughed. "This brown's as thick as I've seen in a long time. Four pounds anyway. Buggers are the best at the right time when they sink down and dredge the bottom. The big ones can't resist."

I followed his lead, casting downriver and across from him, stripping the Bugger, perhaps too rapidly, but I was immediately into a good trout that turned out to be a brown just short of 20 inches. Using Buggers for the remainder of the float, we caught a number of sizable browns, rainbows, and one fat westslope cutthroat.

From that point forward, I worked on learning how to use Woolly Buggers, a process that didn't take long. I soon was catching large trout, and as the years sped by, I refined the process to the point where no matter where or when or what the conditions in Montana, I've always caught at least a pair of trout, usually browns, using the Bugger. I'm convinced that it is the best, most consistent big brown pattern there is. No exceptions.

Bugger Beginnings

The Woolly Bugger had its embryonic beginnings in Harrisburg, Pennsylvania, when fly tier Russell Blessing added a marabou tail to a

The Woolly Bugger in all its ragged glory.

Woolly Worm fly, an addition that helped suggest a swimming movement as the fly was retrieved through the water. He found that even if
fished dead-drift, the fly still had movement.

The Woolly Worm itself is a very old fly that can be found in
Izaak Walton's 1653 book, *The Compleat Angler*. Walton mentions palmered flies, which is a form of "dressing," or building, a fly. A hackle
is wound the length of the hook, usually starting from the rear and
working forward.

Woolly Worm flies go by many names and include a range of
"species." There are permutations by the dozens, including black
Woolly Worms, olive Woolly Worms, and the most interesting, Hot
Butts and Egg-Sucking Leeches. The bead-head version is often com-
posed of a gold bead, the middle section is chenille in an appropriate
color, and the tail may be made from red fibers.

Blessing's original Woolly Bugger had a black marabou tail and a
black-hackled olive chenille body. He had designed it to fish the smallmouth bass in the streams near his home, and had been trying to
imitate the dobsonfly lava. Back in 1967 on a hot August afternoon,
fly-fishing writer Barry Beck was having a hard time getting the fish
to bite on the Little Lehigh River in Pennsylvania. Other fly fishermen
nearby were also having the same problem . . . that is, all except
one. In a thirty-minute period, Russ Blessing netted four nice trout.
Beck went over and asked what fly he was using. It was a streamer.
This type of fly normally was not very productive on the Lehigh River,
especially in August. Blessing gave Beck one of his Woolly Buggers to
try. He started to catch trout.

Beck published an article on Blessing's Woolly Bugger in 1984.
The Bugger is now a standby in fly fishing. Woolly Buggers catch trout,
bass, and salmon in both Atlantic and Pacific rivers, steelhead, arctic
char, northern pike, bluegills, and even carp. I've taken browns on the
pattern from Montana to Alberta to Wisconsin, Iceland, Morocco, and
the rivers of what was once known as Yugoslavia. This wide-ranging

This streambed is good substrate for spawning browns lurking in the shadows of this undercut, overgrown bank.

Never cast to browns that are on or active near their redds, like this one. They are creating trout for future years.

success is due to the fact that these flies can be used to imitate a variety of fish food forms, including baitfish, crustaceans, insect nymphs,
salamanders, and leeches.

Woolly Buggers are tied in green, red, olive, gray, grizzly, brown,
black, yellow, white, and purple, and in all combinations of these colors. I use almost to exclusivity a Cree-hackled, brown-bodied design
that I evolved over the years, with a black marabou tail and body tied
bushy and ratty and weighted with 0.030 wire along the mid-upper
half of the hook shank to aid in sinking the thing and also to give the
Bugger a more lifelike action when retrieved. This fly cannot be hack-
led too densely or tied too ugly.

Bugger Techniques

The Woolly Bugger is my favorite pattern. I've used it to take browns
all over the country, throughout Canada, and in a number of countries
in Africa and Europe. There is nothing like the aggressive take of a big
fish on a Bugger working beneath the surface—the buzz is wild, electric, primitive. There are three main ways I fish the pattern, and while
variations on the Bugger are endless (a guide friend uses a green-
bodied, blue-hackled, sparkle-blue-tailed version while another prefers
all black), I stick to the brown-bodied, Cree-hackled, black-tailed tie that
has taken countless big browns for me over the years. Is this one any
better than all the others? I think so, but productivity is partly a function of faith and time spent in the water searching for fish.

The first method is to cast the Bugger bank-tight or even into the
bank and pull the fly until it drops into the river. If I'm not hanging up or
losing a fly or two, I'm not fishing where the browns are. A difference
of 6 inches or less, from an undercut or overhanging bank, can make
all the difference in terms of success. After the pattern hits the water
(and I prefer the thing to hit with a plop to attract the attention of a big
fish—if it scares off a trout, it's not my kind of brown), I retrieve the
fly with rapid strips of 3 to 6 inches. By rapid I mean as quickly as a

This is true trophy brown Bugger water, but good luck keeping a large fish out of the logjam.

frightened minnow or sculpin might flee a dangerous area or scramble across the streambed. Watch how minnows move in the water you're working to gauge the correct speed.

I prefer to fish the Bugger at least a foot below the surface and often near the bottom. This sometimes requires the addition of one or two AB-size split shot in deep or fast runs. This is not pretty casting, but it works. Nor is it artful like casting small dries. The art is in consistently hitting tight to the bank and in the relentless upstream working of each segment of prime-looking water. For me one cast, at most two, is plenty for each spot. If the Bugger lands tight to cover, it will grab the notice of a brown. And as spawning time nears in the fall, the trout will savagely attack anything near where they're holding. In the summer I've had many browns take the Bugger before it hit the water, perhaps taking the pattern for a grasshopper, a large cricket, or even a small mouse.

The second method is to make the same cast but retrieve the Bugger in slow, shorter strips of maybe 2 to 3 inches with slight pauses in between. This style works best on days that are not overcast but not cloudless, times when the fish are wary and not being territorially aggressive or actively feeding below the surface. Just think of the first method in terms of a vinyl record playing at a speed of 78 rpm (an old Benny Goodman album), this moderate approach as 45 rpm (the Beach Boys), and the following technique at 33⅓ rpm (Quick Silver Messenger Service).

> . . . as spawning time nears in the fall, the trout will savagely attack anything near where they're holding.

The more I fish a Woolly Bugger, the more I use the third method, the dead drift. It seems to take browns more consistently. When the pattern is dead-drifted it imitates a large nymph, perhaps a stonefly, or an injured hopper or forage fish, and just plain looks good to eat. Its slower pace makes for easy prey. Make the same cast and then instead of a stripping retrieve, allow the Bugger to work through a run and then swing out below you. Keep the lightest contact with the fly as possible, with slight adjustments of the line to counteract current and change position of the imitation as it works downstream.

The stream, weather conditions, and mood of the day will dictate the method, or perhaps some blending of the techniques.

All of this looks to be straightforward, and it is on the surface. Initially this is easy to master, but as time passes and empirical experience grows, subtle layers of intuitiveness appear in your fishing—not just in how to work the Woolly Bugger, but in detecting when a brown is closing in or taking with a subtlety that would make a Henry's Fork small-fly-sipping big trout proud. There are times when I can sense that a big fish is around the Bugger and I'll react accordingly by slowly decreasing or increasing the pace of the retrieve depending on "feel." Or I'll make a quick cast to the same location.

Brown Trout Radar

One aspect of fishing for big browns that I've never heard anything about is the awareness that truly large fish have of being hunted. It's analogous to saying, "I felt the hair stand up on my neck, and when I turned around a weird guy was staring at me." Believe what you will, we communicate in some ways that have not yet been quantified. And as any skilled hunter knows (and seeking large browns is truly hunting), animals sense when they are in the presence of a predator and being stalked. I've often thought that it may have something to do with their lateral line system, a network of mechanoreceptors that they use to detect the energy of waves passing over and around their bodies.

In any case, when I'm working along a trout stream and enjoying the experience in a relatively relaxed, serene fashion, when I concentrate on making the right presentation and am enjoying watching a good drift through prime holding water, the big trout come, aren't put down by a feeling that the scales are standing up along their dorsal fins. Instead of racing from spot to spot, casting like the wild man of

This is a perfect Bugger run for big browns.

Always look for big trout where springs and small streams enter a river.

Borneo hell-bent on hammering every big brown in a 1-mile stretch of river, I have a more profound fishing experience, and I also catch more and bigger fish.

The Type of Split Shot Makes a Difference

One aspect of weighting large patterns, particularly those that benefit from a retrieve, relates to the type of split shot I use. For years I used the expensive green, egg-shaped shot that looks cool. The stuff sinks a fly down to the bottom well, and I've caught a lot of very fine fish with this type of weight. For a backup, I also kept a small bag of similarly sized shot by Eagle Claw, though they are lead-colored and not the spiffy shape of the green ones. They also have flared extensions at one end that are used to remove the shot from the tippet by pressing them so the mouth gapes open. I avoided using this brand for a long time because I preferred the streamlined product. But then one day while killing time on a long drive up toward Peerless (I knew it was a long trip because Ginny was asleep and I was comparing split shot), I considered the results with both types of weight. What I realized surprised me. I'd consistently taken more and larger trout with Eagle Claw. By larger, I mean a couple of inches at least. Why, I wasn't sure, but obviously it was a design issue.

After we arrived at the river, I rigged two rods with identical 8-foot leaders tapering to 3X. I attached a #6 Woolly Bugger to each, and then attached the green egg shot at the head of one, and the not-as-hip Eagle Claw to the other. I waded into a wide, pond-like cut bank and cast 30 feet of line with the egg-shaped outfit, retrieved, and closely observed the action. The Bugger dipped and bobbed with each strip and pause, coming steadily and smoothly back to me.

Then I cast the Eagle Claw–weighted Bugger and repeated the process. As the Bugger neared I noticed the expected dip and bob, but what I also thought I saw was a slight shuddering or vibration of the pattern. I went to my knees and cast again and, yes, when the Bugger

Foam lines running along grassy, undercut banks with deep water hold big browns.

came close, I could distinctly see the pattern vibrating slightly side to side. I realize that staring with my face inches from the surface of a river in the middle of nowhere Montana looking for slight differences in the action of an ugly fly pattern might be cause for confinement in more refined areas of our country, but the quest for knowledge often takes curious twists and turns.

It was obvious from this initial experiment that the Eagle Claw split shot imparted a slight bit of motion to the Bugger that made it appear more attractive, more lifelike, to fish. The remainder of the season I fished both types of shot equally in the same stretches of rivers, and the results bordered on definitive. On the same water where I took six browns that averaged 19 inches using green egg-shaped shot, I averaged eleven browns of just over 21 inches using Eagle Claw. This translates to more than a half-pound increase in average weight in addition to higher numbers. I firmly believe that the slight quivering motion imparted to the Bugger or any other streamer is more enticing to large trout. This is the only difference in action I've noticed. I doubt that shot shape or color difference from dull green to dull gray would account for the catch rate and size difference.

If someone had told me a few years ago that this would be the case, I would have said that they were full of it. Today I would emphatically agree with them. I now use Eagle Claw shot exclusively. The correct name for the preferred weight is Eagle Claw Non-lead Removable Shot.

Streamer Patterns

My feelings for Woolly Buggers are strongly positive, but there are several other streamers I use, each for its own reasons. I will always maintain that if I was allowed just one pattern, that pattern would be the Cree-Hackled Woolly Bugger, but the following ties would also work.

The Grey Ghost

The Grey Ghost streamer was first tied in 1924 by Carrie G. Stevens of Madison, Maine. Stevens was the wife of Maine guide Wallace Stevens. During her free time, she tied many other flies in a style known as the Rangeley style. Most of her streamers have in common the use of jungle cock cheeks. The Grey Ghost is regarded as one of her best creations. When Stevens went to the Upper Dam Pool to test it out, she quickly hooked a 6-pound, 13-ounce brookie. She entered the fish in a *Field & Stream* competition, and took second prize.

I remember fishing with Silvio Calabi in May 1990 in the Paradise Valley while attending the Orvis Guides and Outfitters Rendezvous. At the time he was publisher of *Fly Rod & Reel*. We were casting to large rainbows on a mountain lake just north of Yellowstone Park. A mid-afternoon mist swept up from the valley, turning the landscape surreal with whiteout. The fishing was easy for 3- to 7-pound trout that took anything in front of them. This was, after all, a well-managed lake at a high-end, Orvis-endorsed lodge. Silvio looked around, taking in the eerie surroundings, and said, "This would be a great time for a Grey Ghost on this water." He happened to have one. He tied it on and a fat rainbow hit the streamer on the first strip, the silvery white minnow imitation having covered less than 2 feet before the trout swallowed it and ran away just below the surface. The fish were strong fighters, but they had nowhere to run or hide, and always would up being netted and released. The pattern took several more fish before we called a halt to the proceedings and headed for the bar in the main lodge.

Since then I've used the Grey Ghost with some success for big browns, but only on large rivers. The pattern seems to put off or even spook the fish on smaller streams. Just fish it like it was alive and healthy and swimming around with not a care in the world. In big water, browns will take.

Brushy overhangs and undercut banks are tough to fish, but if you aren't losing
Buggers every now and then, you aren't really trying.

The Black-Nosed Dace

The Black-Nosed Dace is a streamer pattern meant to imitate minnows, hence its name. I like to tie this pattern with a half-dozen wraps of 0.020 wire, starting halfway up the shank. The pattern works in smaller rivers and down deep as well. I prefer it to the Grey Ghost.

In 1947 *Art Flick's Streamside Guide* listed only one bucktail, the Black-Nose Dace. There is a good deal of disagreement concerning what the fly represents, with Flick claiming it "resembles chubs, dace, and a host of small minnows that have the dark lateral line down their side."

Flick said that there are two species of minnows that trout feed on, *Rhinichthys atratulus* and *Semotilus atromaculatus*. While the local names vary for these minnows, Flick claimed he had found them on every trout stream he ever fished. Neither of the species exceed 3½ inches in length and are most commonly called Black-Nose Dace. "Because the Black-Nose Dace is so well liked by trout," Flick said, "I tried to imitate it as closely as possible with a bucktail. The result is one that has proved itself successful, as well as one that will take a lot of abuse."

The Mouse That Roars

While it's hard for some beginning brown trout fishermen to believe, big browns will often eat mice that have fallen into the river through a misstep along the bank.

There are a number of mouse patterns out there, but I've found that the Mouse Rat by Dave Whitlock is a good one. I've seen browns appear like magic, cutting a V-wake as they charged this pattern tossed against an undercut bank and allowed to plop into the water. On one river the largest fish I'd taken at the time was 9 pounds. The mouse I threw attracted a male at dusk that was close to twice that size. I hooked the monster, but he simply turned downstream and broke me off in submerged roots 100 feet away. Making the pattern splash and

Forrest Glover, trophy brown trout fisherman extraordinaire, shows what fishing large streamers can sometimes produce. Photo by Forrest Glover

struggle in the retrieve will either draw a vicious attack or send the brown running for cover.

Big trout on the Missouri, Yellowstone, and Teton have all pounced on the mouse. I landed one brown over 10 pounds while standing knee deep in a sucking muck that smelled like rotten eggs along a slow, slightly turbid stretch of the Teton, a handful of miles east of Choteau. It's a good thing that the brown was sluggish, because after I measured his length and girth and admired him, it took me fifteen minutes to drag myself to shore. The suction was so bad, I lost a wading shoe. The fish was just short of 30 inches and weighed, according to a trout calculator, 11.7 pounds, but I haven't been back. The experience was down and dirty at best.

These Are Big Fish Patterns

All of these streamers and, of course, the Woolly Bugger imitate forage fish, small minnows that feed on detritus, tiny insect larvae, and any other miniscule food source. Large browns feed on smaller fish a good deal. The best times are in low light or even at night, though I no longer fish in the dark. The rivers I like are treacherous to wade when visibility is poor. And I like to see the water I'm fishing, along with the fight itself and the end result, of course.

Some people will tell you that enormous browns feed exclusively at night, but that's false information. I've caught them at all hours of the day in all light conditions. The right pattern with the right technique will take trout. Successfully imitating forage fish is why these large patterns are successful. The Woolly Bugger, and the others, also trigger the predatory response that makes trophy browns such an intriguing quarry. When you catch a 6- or 7-pound brown on a Bugger, you understand why some of us are hopelessly addicted to this type of fishing.

Cree-Hackled Woolly Bugger

Hook: Sizes 2–8 or 3X–4X long

Thread: Black 3/0 nylon

Tail: Black marabou, about ⅔ hook
length

Body: Brown chenille

Weight: 0.030 lead wire, 10–12
wraps tied in center-forward, leav-
ing room to wrap head

Hackle: Cree, Howard Hackle grade
2 or 3

Note: Tie this one as bushy and ugly
as possible. Think how a shirt would
look after being dragged behind a
1949 Dodge pickup in a gravel park-
ing lot outside a bar for 40 minutes
after closing time.

Sculpin

Hook: Streamer, sizes 2–6

Thread: Brown 6/0

Ribbing: Fine copper, gold, or silver
wire

Body: Tan chenille or dubbed tan rab-
bit fur, tapered tan floss, etc.

Gills (optional): A few turns of red
chenille or red yarn, red fur dubbing, red floss, etc.

Wing: 4–6 matched dyed brown grizzly saddle hackles. If the feathers
are sparsely barbed, you'll need 6;
if they're heavily barbed, 4.

Head: Dyed brown deer hair clipped
to shape and brown dyed ostrich or
peacock herl for tuft at top of head

Grey Ghost

Hook: TMC 300, size 2

Thread: Black 8/0 UNI-Thread with red band at head

Tag: Small flat silver tinsel

Rib: Small flat silver tinsel

Body: Pumpkin UNI-Stretch

Underwing: White bucktail

Lower wing: White bucktail and peacock herl

Wing: Gray hackles, back to back

Throat: Crest

Sides: Silver pheasant

Cheeks: Jungle cock

Black-Nosed Dace

Hook: Mustad 3665A, 9575, or 38941, sizes 4–12

Thread: Black silk, monochord, or nylon

Tag: Red yarn, very short

Body: Flat silver tinsel

Wing: Lower third: polar bear or white impala. Middle third: black skunk or black bear. Top third: brown bucktail.

Head: Black silk

Mouse Rat,
originated by Dave Whitlock

Hook: TMC 8089, sizes 2–10

Thread: Back: white 3/0. Front: black 3/0.

Body: Natural deer

Tail: Tan chamois

Head: Natural deer

Eyes: Black Pantone

Note: For whiskers, use black moose; for ears, use the same as the tail.

Optional: Use heavy monofilament tied from eye to curve for weedless version.

CHAPTER 7

Final Thoughts

A trout is a moment of beauty known only to those who seek it.
—Arnold Gingrich

Early October is when large browns lose their secretive, shadowy behavior. The trout, driven by the spawning urge, roam the shallow gravel runs where the females will build their redds in earnest in a week or so. Most times browns are secretive, loners. Even the chaotic splash of a suicidal grasshopper a few feet out in the open water rarely causes them to move. Nymphs, minnows, smaller trout, any of these that happen to wander in front of the large predators will be killed quickly, but otherwise they won't budge.

I want to connect, to feel a wild fish as it runs for cover at the bite of the hook or walks and crashes along the surface. The trout's fight for survival makes me feel alive. Perhaps a cruel way to get one's kicks, but I'm a predator, too—an emotional one above all else.

So after taking a half-dozen browns, a small brook trout, and a Yellowstone cutthroat, everything is pretty much as I've always remembered it over the years. The stream is low and clear. The leaves on willows, birches, and cottonwoods are going brilliant yellow, manipulating light in carefree ways. Strings of geese are moving

The best of all things fly fishing—a fine October day and an isolated stream filled
with brown trout.

south with their common cries. The last dregs of this year's mayflies bounce above the river's surface. Ahead I see an oval depression of newly cleared stone. The first brown trout spawning bed. One of many that will be dotted along this isolated stretch of water before much longer.

Yeah, all of this seems the same, but just like the end of last season and the one before and so on, everything is different in ways that are visible, but not to the eyes. This valley and everywhere else I travel in Montana at this time of the year seems to have shifted to a slightly different slice of time than the one I'm buzzing in. There's just enough of this movement to make me feel as though I'm in the middle of the gentlest of earthquakes or passing through a mild moment of dizziness. I feel like I'm in a room where the furniture has been subtly rearranged with such sophistication that I can't notice the changes.

> Brown trout have an attitude, a bad-ass approach to life that takes no prisoners.

Words from Someone Who Knows

Brown trout have an attitude, a bad-ass approach to life that takes no prisoners. This attribute attracts a certain breed of fly fisher. One of the best on the planet is an individual from Tennessee, Forrest Glover. As his pictures emphatically demonstrate, Forrest knows how to take very large brown trout. I connected with Forrest on the Classic Fly Rod Forum (http://clarksclassicflyrodforum.yuku.com), a tremendous site for information on bamboo rods, reels, and related information. On a thread about J. W. Young and Dingley reels, I came across Forrest and checked out his profile. His brown trout photographs blew me away. I contacted him to see if he would share some of his angling information, and he was more than generous with his time, photos, and knowledge.

"Thanks for the interest!" said Glover. "Let's just say that I have spent countless hours chasing trout, and I have learned a tremendous amount, but one simple thing comes to mind. It may sound stupid

Forrest Glover and one of his enormous browns. Photo by Forrest Glover

but if you want to catch trophy fish you have to fish where there are trophies to be caught.

"For me on the East Coast, the best chance at trophies, and I mean monster trout, are tailwater fisheries and the Great Lakes. I have caught numerous large trout below hydroelectric dams and tailwaters. In the right ecosystem these fish can grow to enormous sizes and can be targeted by fishermen. Though I have not fished all of these, a few come to mind like the White River and the Little Red River in Arkansas. Most all the Tennessee Valley Authority hydro dams like the South Holston, Wautauga, Hiwassee, Clinch, Caney Fork, and others have trophy trout.

"Probably the best opportunity at a trout over 10 pounds without having to fly to Terra Del Fuego or some exotic location is the Great Lakes. Every fall there is a huge migration of salmonids, and the trout love to follow them upriver and gorge themselves on eggs. These trout are already large from feeding on baitfish in the lakes, but then a steady diet of eggs puts some weight on them as well. Now it comes to a point in these situations where angling ethics has to enter the conversation because the trout will go on a spawn of their own shortly after the salmon start dying off the beds, and they will just use the same beds for their own spawn. If a person times it correctly they can fish for these fish before and after the spawn and not harass them while it is going on. Everyone has different feelings on the subject and it is very controversial so it is probably one you may not want to tackle in your book." Fishing while the trout are on their redds is never acceptable, but this is not what Glover is talking about. This "to fish or not to fish" decision is up to the individual fly fisher.

"However," Glover continued, "the change that starts happening in a brown before and after a spawn makes them a lot easier to catch during this time period for numerous reasons. First off, these large fish have left their hiding spots in the deeper holes of a stream or the safety of a huge lake. They are now not as scared to come up into

Once more with feeling. Photo by Forrest Glover

shallow runs and shoals where they would normally never go. This now gives the angler an opportunity. The other thing is that I believe these fish become very nocturnal during the spring and summer and will hardly feed during the normal fishing times of an angler, so you have to take advantage of the seasons and capitalize on their availability and eagerness to feed. Browns become very aggressive in the early fall and are really starting to pack on some weight preparing for the spawn.

"They become very opportunistic eaters and eat things during this time that I feel they don't normally eat during most of the year. For example, I have caught numerous browns over 10 lbs on small nymphs (#16 and smaller), but I know that they did not get to 10 lbs or larger feeding on a bunch of little insects. They are eating meat and other larger sources of protein, but during this time just before and after a spawn they seem to want to eat almost anything that resembles a viable food source. Of course this is not always the case, but I have found that I have greater success on large trout and my smaller flies during the early fall time of the year.

"During the rest of the seasons, these fish can be caught, but are much more keen and are going to be looking for a much more substantial meal. In some areas like the Great Lakes, and also with some of these tailwater fisheries, the large fish have moved out or down into the lake and are not even around to be caught by the angler. I have had numerous questions about those pictures from forum members. Many want specific streams and dates and flies, etc. But a fisherman has to keep some secrets."

Fishing Alone

I've never been much for fishing with guides or doing the in-thing like traveling to the latest hot river or lodge. I'm a true loner, like the browns, and simpler is better. It avoids confusion and eventual torment. Those who have patiently guided me along a life that revolves

What all of this is about—beautiful water, solitude, and big browns.

A healthy brown taken from a tiny spring out on the high plains that was so narrow, I could jump across it as I worked upstream.

around good country have all said in their own curious ways, "That's cool that you made that cast that caught that fish, but that's not what's important. What counts, kid, is that river you're standing in. Those mountains over there. That blood-red prairie we crossed at sunrise—how all of it makes you feel. That's the game you're really after."

And I finally grasped the natural concept. Basically it's brain-dead simple. Lose the ego. Submit to the land. Connect with the feral buzz, then recognize my insignificant yet worthwhile place in the untamed, unfathomable scheme of things. None of the good stuff is related to fancy clothing, pricey fly rods, or $5,000-a-week lodge gigs. Get wet and a little muddy. Then feel good enough to slide along in a strange dance for no good reason.

In addition to large, native Yellowstone cutthroat, there are quite a few big browns in this wilderness stream on the northern flanks of the Absaroka Mountains. The outside bend in the center of the photograph always yields a good-size trout or two (at least that's what Flea of the Red Hot Chili Peppers told me).

The light of October is special. It glows with an amber influence. I look up from my tree-trunk seat and spot a brown holding in a soft run about 40 feet upstream. Only its fins and slight flicks of its tail reveal motion. Slowly I work out line to cover the distance, then make the cast and start the retrieve. The fish hits the pattern with its head once, then again. It circles back and slams the streamer. The white of its mouth flashes. This fish thrashes across the surface, tires quickly, and comes easily to me as I kneel in a few inches of water. Reds, browns, blacks, pale greens, and bronze flanks. The lower jaw is formed into a kype. A male. Over 27 inches and nearly 7 pounds. I twist the hook free and watch as the trout swims slowly across stream to a deep hole beneath the tangled roots of an old cottonwood. My fragile, lunatic world shifts casually out of kilter. I'm a bit afraid, then serene again, then laughing. "Completely nuts, Holt," I say out loud to no one, and feel good about it.

Appendix A:
Choice Quality Stuff

I tie all of my flies and make a point of using quality hackle, but feather prices are getting absurdly high. Howard Hackle's prices are the best for top-notch hackle, and their service is excellent (www.howard hackle.com). I love Cree, but no matter where I go, the price is high. Such is life.

I've been using Dr. Slick hackle clamps, scissors, and fly-tying tools for a long time. Fine craftsmanship, quality materials, and a good feel to boot from the boys in Belgrade, Montana (www.drslick.com).

You can debate which is the best fly line forever. I've used Cortland 444 Peach and Sylk lines for years. The WF (weight-forward) lines cast hard, fast, and accurately, and the DT (double-taper) items make mending and roll casting a breeze. I have a Sylk DT2 on a Hardy St. George Junior and it's a marvel to use. Cortland's backing and leaders are good, too (www.cortlandline.com).

Jim Teeny makes my favorite sink-tip lines (www.jimteeny.com). I especially like their weight-forward mini tip lines that come in sizes 3 to 9.

TroutHunter nylon tippet and leaders are at the top of my list right now (www.trouthunt.com). Supple, strong, consistent, and the tippet is also available in 4.5X, 5.5X, and 6.5X—a very nice feature.

Rio (www.rioproducts.com) and Stroft (www.stroft.de) make excellent lightweight tippet material, sold by many fly shops. Fluorocarbon seems too stiff to allow natural motion of my flies.

For weighting Woolly Buggers and large nymphs, Eagle Claw non-lead removable sinkers are my choice for the reasons discussed in the body of this book (www.eagleclaw.com). Not as fancy as the green egg-shaped shot, but more effective.

A small brown trout complements a vintage Hardy Perfect reel.

Quantum Hot Sauce reel grease and oil is the best lubricant around. The stuff is formulated to molecularly bond with all metal parts, and it protects under a variety of rough conditions, including cold water and weather. It is long-lasting and won't turn stiff or tar-like. It costs more, over $10 with shipping per tube, but it's worth it (www.quantumfishing.com).

Boeshield T-9 is an excellent lubricant and protectant for reels. The spray will also loosen frozen nuts and reel spindles. The formulation, based on a unique combination of solvents and waxes, is designed to penetrate metal pores and dissolve minor corrosion, then leave a resilient waxy coating that lasts for months. About $10 per bottle (http://boeshield.com).

I use Renaissance Wax to clean up and protect old reels (though caution is advised because it is mildly abrasive and will remove some finishes). I've even used it as a final protection for my bamboo rods after polishing. It's expensive— $15 plus shipping for 2.25 ounces— but worth it (www.restorationproduct.com).

For polishing old bamboo rods and also slightly improving rough finishes, I use all of the grades of Brownells rubbing compound, working from the roughest needed to the finest, which is Triple "F." Order all at once to save on the pricey shipping costs. About $11 for a 2-ounce tub (www.brownells.com; search "rubbing compound").

There are dozens of fine reels on the market. My preference is for vintage reels like the Hardy Perfects made by Wilf Sinton or the Farlow, J. W. Young, and Dingley Perfects. I also have a soft spot in my heart and a hole in my wallet for the original reels designed by Ari Hart—great pieces that are as functional as they are beautiful. I'm also looking for West Coast–made, fifty-year-old, Thompson 100, 200, and 500 reels, but that's another costly tale. Of current build, I just bought a new Hardy St. George and, in addition to being a solid reel, it is a work of art (http://fly.hardyfishing.com).

When it comes to rods, I'm obsessed with vintage bamboo—Granger, Payne, Leonard, Heddon, Edwards, Phillipson, Constable, Young, and even Montague, Horrocks & Ibbotson, and Abbey & Imbrie. I've got around fifty, with many more flickering on the near horizon. It's an addiction, but then life without addictions is a life unlived. Believe me, I know.

My favorite fly boxes are made by Hardy. The vintage Neroda boxes that were made eighty years ago are works of art. They cost a bunch, but are worth the money. You can find them for auction on eBay. The newer replicas by Hardy are available at Vintage Fishing Tackle (www.vintagefishingtackle.co.uk). These are very nice, but they aren't the original item. Orvis used to make clear plastic, compartmentalized fly boxes sealed with a rubber gasket. The compartments were formed by removable dividers that allowed an angler to vary the size of the compartments. Whenever I see them—on eBay, in secondhand stores, at yard sales—I snap them up.

I avoid wearing waders whenever I can, but Simms (www.simmsfishing.com) has come up with a product that makes the wader experience not only bearable for the likes of me, but even enjoyable. Their GS3 GuidePant is just that. Gor-Tex construction that is DEET resistant, and they even have lined hand pockets. Worth the money.

Most of the time when it's warm, and even when it's not, I wade wearing a shirt with long sleeves like those made by Ex Officio, jeans or cutoffs, and wading sandals like the Streamtread Sandal by Simms, by far the best I've found to date.

Ginny and I spend a lot of time out in the sun, wind, and bugs, so we're always looking for the best sun-care products. Tropical Seas (www.tropicalseas.com) is the best we've found—biodegradable, long-lasting, and also reasonably priced. Their Reef Safe backcountry sunscreen is SPF 30 and uses citronella to repel insects. Admittedly, in places like the Yukon or out on the high plains during late spring, even a cloud of DEET would help only marginally, but under reasonably sane conditions, Reef Safe is the real deal. Their Burn Cooler, Rehydrating Gel, Expedition repellent, and straight sunscreen are also excellent.

Every fly fisher has a favorite pair of sunglasses. Mine are Ray-Ban Wayfarers in both dark GL-15 XLT and the brown tint, depending on light conditions (www.ray-ban.com/usa). I'm one of those clowns who don't notice much, if any, difference using polarized or non-polarized lenses. Go figure.

I love knives and have dozens of them, but most often carry a Schrade's Hunting & Fishing Knife made in the 1940s, engraved with a swordfish and moose. I like older stuff. Buck Knives makes a very handy item called the X-Tract Fin that is like a Swiss Army Knife only slimmer (www.buckknives.com).

Can't live without flashlights. Streamlight (www.streamlight.com) makes a headlamp that is handy and indispensable early in the day and around dusk and beyond. Their flashlights are also excellent—really bright focused light, dependable, and heavy-duty.

Much of the fishing Ginny and I do involves camping. We've discovered some items that work well for us and are a cut above similar equipment. The Brunton Two-Burner Profile Stove is by far the best designed, constructed, and operational model we've ever used. It is safe and easy to use, and heats food and water fast. It is available at numerous sites online.

The idea of dealing with the claustrophobia associated with so-called bivouac or expedition tents that have all the ambiance of a pizza oven is abhorrent to us. The REI Mountain 3 tent is spacious and airy. It handles the weather, including wind, well and is easy to set up and well made. It costs $399, so it's an investment, but a worthwhile one (www.rei.com).

When we're not using the REI down bags we each purchased over thirty-five years ago, we use Phantom sleeping bags that weigh in at less than 1.5 pounds and are good down to 20 degrees (www.mountainhardwear.com). These are especially handy on trips into the hills or down the Yellowstone where weight and space are issues.

One of the best purchases we ever made in the camping arena was the Coleman Cooking Station Table. This item makes life in camp a lot easier and convenient. It weighs 22 pounds, but so what? I did the Spartan trip decades ago where I pulled on my Barbour wax-cotton poncho filled with a pint of Jim Beam, a pack of Camel straights, a few cans of beer, flashlight, and mentions, then rolled under my pickup and went to sleep. This was all well and cute when I was twenty-five, but I prefer comfort to false extremism these days. The table costs $95.95 (www.summitcampinggear.com).

Finally, some of the fly-fishing magazines I read are *The Fly Fish Journal* (www.theflyfishjournal.com), *Fly Rod & Reel* (www.flyrodreel.com/magazine), and *Waterlog* (www.waterlogmagazine.com). This last one is printed in England and venerates the eccentricity that is the British approach not only to angling but to life as well, as if there is a difference.

Appendix B:
Guides and Outfitters in Brown Trout Country

To direct anglers to reputable operations as well as to give them a jumping-off point for their trophy brown trout adventures, I offer the following list of guides, outfitters, and services relating to brown trout. The list, of course, is by no means complete or definitive. There are hundreds, if not thousands, of highly qualified individuals and businesses around the world that will take a fly fisher into the heart of brown trout country, whether it be in Montana, Vermont, Iceland, Argentina, Tasmania, or Morocco. A number of these outfits, as it turns out, are Orvis-endorsed. I've had a solid relationship with Orvis, especially Tom Rosenbauer, for a quarter century, and I trust their recommendations. It should also be mentioned that I'm not getting paid for these selections, not a dime. When you see an Aston Martin DB in front of my place, you'll know I've gone over to the other side. I've also relied on Frontiers Travel for worldwide listings.

Frontiers Travel
PO Box 959
Wexford, PA 15090-0959
(800) 245-1950
info@frontierstravel.com
www.frontierstravel.com
Founded in 1969, Frontiers specializes in worldwide fly-fishing and shooting destinations. They have a combined staff of seventy-five in their Wexford, Pennsylvania, headquarters and UK branch office. Anywhere you might want to fish can more than likely be made real by Frontiers. A number of my friends have arranged trips through Frontiers, and they all have had good experiences. They've been around for years and are as good as it gets.

United States

EASTERN

Breadloaf Mountain Lodge and Fly Shop
Cornwall Bridge, CT 06754
(860) 672-6064
www.flyfishct.com
Fly fishing in New England is available through the Breadloaf Mountain Lodge and Fly Shop. They're located on the Housatonic River in Connecticut, and offer full-service guided wade and drift trips. Full- and half-day trips are available.

Harrison Anglers
Shelburn Falls, MA 01370
(413) 222-6207
www.harrisonanglers.com
Harrison runs float trips for trophy browns and rainbows on all 40 miles of the Deerfield River in western Massachusetts. This classic tailwater stretches from the Berkshires to the Connecticut River Valley. Fishing for truly large browns is available all year.

Richie Bernard
Waterville Valley, NH 03215
(603) 434-2193
flyfishnh@ymail.com
www.finfighters.com
Orvis-endorsed fly-fishing guide Richie Bernard will take you fishing for trophy trout in near-wilderness settings, including the ponds and rivers surrounded by the White Mountains of New Hampshire.

West Branch Angler Sportsman's Resort
150 Faulkner Rd.
Hancock, NY 13783
(800) 201-2557 or (607) 467-5525
wbangler@westbranchangler.com
www.westbranchresort.com
This New York fly-fishing resort features twenty-six newly renovated, modern log cabins on the banks of the West Branch of the Delaware River. You can fish by drift boat or wading, and on any of the three branches of the Delaware, for wild brown and rainbow trout. The Delaware is one of the East's finest trout streams, and holds good numbers of big browns.

Jones Outfitters, Ltd.
2419 Main St.
Lake Placid, NY 12946
(518) 523-3468
www.jonesoutfitters.com
Jones Outfitters provides a wide range of guided fishing trips. Many anglers choose to fish the West Branch of the Au Sable, but if the water happens to be high, low, or discolored, other quality waters include the Salmon, Saranac, and St. Regis.

Damon Newpher
Bradford, PA 16701
(814) 598-4562
www.pa-flyfishing.com
Damon Newpher specializes in guiding wade and drift boat trips on the Allegheny River tailwaters, Clarion River, and Lake Erie for trophy trout. This is a place to connect with a large brown.

Captain Joe Demalderis
Cross Current Guide Service
Milford, PA 18337
(914) 475-6779
www.crosscurrentguideservice.com
Joe Demalderis, the 2010 Orvis-Endorsed Freshwater Fly-Fishing Guide of the Year, offers fishing on the Upper Delaware River System, which forms the natural border between Pennsylvania and New York. Considered one of the best wild trout fisheries in the country, the Delaware System encompasses up to 80 miles of water that is worked by wading and drift boat. These waters include the Beaverkill, Willowemoc, Neversink, and the East Branch, West Branch, and Main Stem of the Delaware. You could spend several seasons in this country and never fish, let alone learn, all of it.

Thomas E. Baltz
328 Zion Rd.
Mt. Holly Springs, PA 17065
(717) 486-7438
baltzte@aol.com
Baltz offers guiding on south-central Pennsylvania's classic limestone trout streams. Waters include the Letort and Yellow Breeches.

Ben Turpin
Saylorsburg, PA 18353
(570) 807-3027
www.benturpin.com
Offering year-round fly fishing on the classic and revered trout streams of northeast Pennsylvania and New Jersey, either full- or half-day trips are available. He is close to New York City and Philadelphia.

Smoky Mountain Gillies
H. Clay Aalders
Knoxville, TN 37920
(865) 577-4289
www.smokymountaingillies.com
Offering wading trips in Great Smoky Mountains National Park or tailwater floats, Smoky Mountain Gillies can show you wild browns, brook trout, and rainbows in forested mountain surroundings. This is small-stream fishing as it should be—the kind of country that makes me feel like a kid again. Not many trophy browns, but enough to keep your interest.

Cold River Outfitters
111 New Horizons Ln.
Chippenhook, VT 05777
(802) 282-5131
info@coldriveroutfitters.com
www.coldriveroutfitters.com
Cold River offers weekend trips in the Rutland/Killington area—beautiful country with many quality trout waters.

Taconic Guide Service
Manchester, VT 05255
(802) 688-4304
vtangler@live.com
Taconic Guide Service offers drift boat fishing as well as wade fishing in the Battenkill Valley of Vermont and New York. This area is beautiful and contains some of fly fishing's holy waters. I spent many hours fishing with a friend of mine who lived in the region and always caught good-sized trout.

Spikehorn Ridge
PO Box 135
Washington, VT 05675
(802) 233-6621
reillymccue@myfairpont.net
www.spikehornridge.com
Spikehorn has a solid reputation for putting anglers onto brown, brook, rainbow, and lake trout, in addition to landlocked salmon, which are related to browns and a treat to catch on a fly. The operation runs out of the lodge at Spikehorn Ridge. The chance to sink into the landscape via camping trips is another option.

J. M. Knabe
Wilmington, VT 05363
(800) 528-3961
www.taddingers.com
The Upper Deerfield River, where J. M. Knabe guides, contains browns, brookies, rainbows, and landlocked salmon. While the East Branch of the Upper Deerfield is best known for native brook trout deep in the mountains, big browns hang out here, too.

Elk River Guide Service
Highway 219
Slatyfork, WV 26291
(866) 572-3771
ertc@ertc.com
www.ertc.com/guidedflyfishing.htm
Elk River Guide Service can show you West Virginia wild brown, rainbow, and brook trout—all present in good numbers, with some large ones skulking about under the banks. They are located streamside on the limestone-influenced Slaty Fork of the Elk River. Guided trips include the Williams, Cherry, Cranberry, Potomac, Seneca, Blackwater, and Shavers Fork headwaters. There are excellent smallmouth floats on the New, Greenbrier, and James. Open year-round. This is the country the late writer Breece D'J Pancake loved more than life itself.

MIDWESTERN

John Gulley
7232 Highway 101
Gamaliel, AR 72537
(870) 499-7517
fish@flyguide.com
www.flyguide.com
Offering year-round fly fishing on quality Ozark trout streams and lakes, Gulley is an Arkansas native with thirty years' experience in guiding. This guy will put you onto very large browns.

Jamie Rouse Fly-Fishing Adventures
470 Wildflower Rd.
Heber Springs, AR 72543
(501) 250-1275
www.jamierouse.net
Arkansas is home to the former world-record brown trout and plenty of big fish. Trips to the White and Norfork Rivers are available through this year-round fly-fishing guide service based on the Little Red River. This Razorback can put you onto huge browns.

Northeast Iowa Fly Fishing
http://neiflyfishing.com
NEI Fly Fishing is a trout-fishing guide service based in Decorah, which is located in the "driftless region" of northeast Iowa. They offer wading trips on the area's spring-fed creeks. There's some very good brown trout fishing in this part of Iowa. The country, weather, and fishing is very similar to that found in Wisconsin's driftless zone.

Pere Marquette River Lodge
8841 South M-37
Baldwin, MI 49304
(231) 745-3972
www.pmlodge.com
Located on the Pere Marquette River in the "flies-only, no-kill zone," fly fishing doesn't get any better than here. Try to catch the legendary Hex hatch for big browns that feed in the night.

Hawkins Outfitters
Lake Ann, MI 49650
(231) 228-7135
www.hawkinsflyfishing.com
Located near Traverse City, with guiding on rivers in lower northwest Michigan, Hawkins is fully permitted for all rivers, including the Pere Marquette, Manistee, Au Sable, Muskegon, and some lesser-known streams. This is premier fly-fishing country and worth any angler's time.

River Run Outfitters
2626 Highway 165
Branson, MO 65616
(877) 699-3474 or (417) 332-0460
www.riverrunoutfitters.com
River Run Outfitters offers guide services to a section of the White River that's a premier year-round tailwaters fishery, with plenty of rainbow and brown trout over 20 inches.

Dakota Angler & Outfitter
513 Seventh St.
Rapid City, SD 57701
(605) 341-2450
flyfish@rapidnet.com
http://flyfishsd.com/guidedtours.htm
The Black Hills area offers a wide range of opportunities to the fly fisher, with streams that include Rapid, Spring, Box Elder, and Castle Creeks. Browns, brookies, and rainbows are all found in healthy numbers and sizes. The fishing is excellent year-round, although the best months are April through October. The Black Hills remind me of an enormous Montana island mountain group sitting out in the middle of the high prairie.

On the Creek
2120 Main St.
Cross Plains, WI 53528-9596
(608) 798-1137
www.onthecreekflyshop.com
A full-service fly shop that provides guide service to beautiful trout streams near where I grew up decades ago, they can guide you to some nice browns. The fishing is idyllic, to say the least.

Nick Volk
Madison, WI 53705
(608) 449-8278
www.streamsideoutfitters.com
Fish the "driftless region" of southwestern Wisconsin for browns, brookies, and rainbows. I grew up fishing this marvelous country. Even without the browns, this place is heaven. Nick Volk also offers drift boat trips for Lake Michigan tributary spawning-run browns.

WESTERN

Wild Waters Fly Fishing

Mount Shasta, CA (530) 926-3810

www.wildwatersflyfishing.com

The waters around Mount Shasta, California, offer year-round angling for Klamath River steelhead and king salmon, McCloud River rainbows, and German and Loch Leven browns.

Willowfly Anglers

PO Box 339

Almont, CO 81210

(888) 761-FISH (3474) or (970) 641-1303

fish@willowflyanglers.com

www.willowflyanglers.com

Fly fish for wild rainbows, browns, and cutthroats in the mountain streams of Colorado. Stalk trophy rainbows in the Taylor Canyon, cast dry flies at wild trout on the East River, or fish the big riffles and deep pools of the Gunnison River. Colorado fishing at its best.

Bucking Rainbow Outfitters

730 Lincoln Ave.

PO Box 774832

Steamboat Springs, CO 80487

(888) 810-8747 or (970) 879-8747

www.buckingrainbow.com

Bucking Rainbow Outfitters, located in northwest Colorado, provides year-round fly fishing with access to over 60 miles of private water. Their fishing waters include the Yampa, Elk, Little Snake, White, and North Platte Rivers.

North Park Anglers
Walden, CO 80480
(970) 723-4215
www.northparkanglers.com
North Park's only full-service fly shop is located in Walden, in the heart of the basin's diverse fishing opportunities. North Park Anglers can guide you on the headwaters of the North Platte River, including 40 miles of private access and permits on the prime water. The North Platte is one of the West's best big trout streams.

Three Rivers Ranch
PO Box 856, Warm River
Ashton, ID 83420
(208) 652-3750
www.threeriversranch.com
Three Rivers Ranch is a fly-fishing lodge in Idaho that has provided guide service to fly fishers for over thirty-five years. This is one of the best. My late grandmother fished here for years.

Fins & Feathers
81801 Gallatin Rd.
Bozeman, MT 59718
(877) 790-5303
info@finsandfeathersonline.com
www.finsandfeathersonline.com
Fins & Feathers offers float or wade fishing for wild brown trout in southwest Montana. Their waters include the Madison, Yellowstone, Jefferson, Gallatin, and Missouri Rivers.

Hubbard's Yellowstone Lodge

287 Tom Miner Creek Rd.
Emigrant, MT 59027
(406) 848-7755
www.hubya.com/hyl

Set in the mountains above the Paradise Valley, the massive log lodge offers the fly fisherman quality cuisine and fine guest rooms with mountain views. Merrell Lake—an 85-acre spring-fed mountain lake full of trout—is out the front door. Silvio Calabi, Bob Jones, and I had a blast fishing the lake years ago. The Yellowstone River is at the back, and Montana's famous spring creeks and Yellowstone Park are nearby. Classic western brown trout country.

Madison Valley Ranch

307 Jeffers Rd.
Ennis, MT 59729
(800) 891-6158
fishing@madisonvalleyranch.com
www.madisonvalleyranch.com

Situated on the banks of the Madison River just 3 miles north of Ennis, the location offers anglers access to the famous "Channels" section of the Madison (one of my favorites) and Jack Creek as it runs through the property. Daily float trips on the varied sections of the Madison, Yellowstone, Big Hole, Beaverhead, and Gallatin Rivers, and access to Ruby River.

Eagle Nest Lodge

PO Box 509
Hardin, MT 59034
(866) 258-3474 or (406) 665-3711
flyfishmt@sbcglobal.net

Eagle Nest Lodge is famous for its Bighorn fishing, as well as its great wing shooting. This is a high-class operation that I had the pleasure of visiting years ago. I hear it is now better than ever.

Dan Bailey's Fly Shop
209 West Park St.
Livingston, MT 59047
(800) 356-4052
www.dan-bailey.com
This venerable and justly famous business has been in Livingston for over seventy years. Since Dan Bailey opened the shop in 1938, the place has offered flies, goods, and good advice to some of the world's best fly fishers. This store is located in the heart of trophy brown trout country.

Long Outfitting
Mathew Long
PO Box 1224
Livingston, MT 59047
(406) 220-6775
www.longoutfitting.com
With access to the fisheries of the Paradise and Gallatin Valleys, Long Outfitting can guide you on Armstrong's, DePuy's, Nelson's, Benhart's, and Thompson's Spring Creeks, as well as put you in a drift boat on the Yellowstone and Madison Rivers.

Blackfoot River Outfitters
John Herzer and Terri Raugland
Missoula, MT 59808
(406) 542-7411
www.blackfootriver.com
Blackfoot River Outfitters works the Blackfoot along with the Bitterroot, the Clark Fork, Rock Creek, the Smith, and Georgetown Lake (and lesser known creeks). It's possible to catch brown, rainbow, westslope cutthroat, and brook trout on the same day. One- to seven-day trips are available.

Grizzly Hackle Fly Shop
215 West Front St.
Missoula, MT 59802
(800) 297-8996
info@grizzlyhackle.com
www.grizzlyhackle.com
The Grizzly Hackle is an established fly shop and guide service working prime brown trout waters, including the Clark Fork, the Blackfoot, the Bitterroot, and Rock Creek, to name a few. You could spend an entire summer and fall fishing within a 50-mile radius of Missoula. This is as good an outfit as any to do business with in that glorious pursuit.

Blue Damsel Lodge
1081 Rock Creek Rd.
Rock Creek, MT 59825
(866) 875-9909 or (406) 825-3077
info@bluedamsel.com
www.bluedamsel.com
Located on the famous Rock Creek, forty-five minutes from Missoula's airport, the Blue Damsel Lodge offers good fishing for browns and other trout species. I spent many days on this stream in the early seventies when I was supposed to be in class at the University of Montana.

Firehole Ranch
West Yellowstone, MT 59758
(406) 646-7294
www.fireholeranch.com
Firehole Ranch is located minutes from Yellowstone National Park. The 640-acre ranch is nestled along Hebgen Lake and surrounded by national forest. Their waters include the Madison, Yellowstone, Henry's Fork, Firehole, Gallatin, and Lamar—trophy brown streams all. This area is the nexus for quality fly fishing in the West.

Vermejo Park Ranch

Raton, NM 87740

(505) 445-2059

www.vermejoparkranch.com

Vermejo Park Ranch in northeastern New Mexico has twenty-one stocked lakes and 30 miles of stream, providing fishing for brown, rainbow, and brook trout averaging 1 to 2 pounds, with many in the 3- to 8-pound class.

Doc Thompson

PO Box 52

Ute Park, NM 87749

(575) 376-9220

www.flyfishnewmexico.com

Book Doc Thompson and fly fish Taos and northern New Mexico for wild trout in the spring, summer, and fall on mountain streams and pristine canyon rivers. Private waters are also accessible.

Cascade Guides and Outfitters

57100 Mall Dr.

PO Box 3676

Sunriver, OR 97707

(888) 230-HOOK or (541) 593-2358

www.cascadeguides.com

Cascade Guides and Outfitters offers float trips on the Deschutes River for wild brown trout, redside rainbows, or steelhead. There are also more than a hundred lakes and 400 miles of spring creeks, tailwaters, and mountain streams in their area.

Rocky Mountain Outfitters
Heber City, UT 84032
(435) 654-1655
info@rockymtnoutfitters.com
www.rockymtnoutfitters.com
Rocky Mountain Outfitters provides fishing on the Provo River in the shadow of Mount Timpanogos. The Provo River produces large browns and rainbows—a truly fine fishery.

Ugly Bug Fly Shop
240 S. Center St.
Casper, WY 82601
866-UGLYBUG
uglybugflyshop@qwestoffice.net
www.crazyrainbow.net
The Ugly Bug Fly Shop, located in central Wyoming, provides year-round fly fishing along the North Platte River. The "Grey Reef" tailwater along this river is one of the West's best trophy trout fisheries. Their wild browns, rainbows, and cutthroats average 17 to 22 inches.

North Fork Anglers
1107 Sheridan Ave.
Cody, WY 82414
(307) 527-7274
flyfish@wavecom.net
www.northfolkanglers.com
The Cody/Yellowstone area offers 2,500 miles of blue-ribbon trout waters. Wild brown, cutthroat, rainbow, and brook trout average 16 inches and run much larger.

Alberta, Canada

Alberta Fly Fishing Adventures

(877) 363-3258

albertaflyfishing@shaw.ca

www.albertaflyfishing.ab.ca

Alberta Fly Fishing Adventures guides the Crowsnest area where three trout rivers meet—the Oldman, Crowsnest, and Castle. While surrounded by these headwaters and the nearby Waterton River, there are also at least twenty lesser-known trout streams accessible from the shop. I've been fishing this area for more than thirty years and find something new on each visit.

Bow River Adventures

Richard Mason

#10 Drake Landing Way

Okotoks, AB, Canada T1S-0B9

(403) 995-3677 or (403) 978-3674 (cell)

dutchflythebow@yahoo.ca

www.bowriveradventures.com

Bow River Adventures offers float trips for fly fishing as well as walk and wade trips with experienced guides. This outfit is on one of the best trout rivers in the world.

Fly Fish Alberta

(403) 346-1698

info@flyfishalberta.com

www.flyfishalberta.com

Formed in 1996, Fly Fish Alberta offers guided fly-fishing trips from the Bow River in Calgary to the Red Deer River and its tributaries. This can be some of the best brown trout fly fishing outside New Zealand. The Ram River is known mainly for its cutthroat, but is a gorgeous stream every fly fisher should experience.

South America

Rio Manso Lodge, Argentina
(800) 547-4322
OrvisTravel@Orvis.com
Deep in the wilds of Argentinean Patagonia, right in the Andes, Rio Manso Lodge is located on the bank of Lake Hess and the Manso River in Nahuel Huapi National Park. Unlike most of the Argentinean Patagonia operations, which are located on large estancias surrounded by pampas, the Rio Manso Lodge is surrounded by forested national park land. Weather diversity and the scarcity of fishing pressure produce excellent fishing. It is common to catch fish in the 2- to 4-pound range daily, and there is reasonable chance for 5- to 10-pound trout during a week of fishing. They're open mid-December through March.

San Huberto Lodge, Argentina
(800) 547-4322
OrvisTravel@Orvis.com
San Huberto Lodge is set among the rivers flowing east from the volcanic peaks of the Andes. The Patagonian landscape of wide open plains set against a backdrop of high, forested peaks is from another world. From headwaters high in mountain lakes, these cold rivers cut through the pampas, creating ideal conditions for trout. Each river has a distinct personality, and few regions feature the subtle variety of fishing as the land north of Bariloche, the northwestern corner of the Patagonian region. This is the land popularized by angling legends such as Joe Brooks and Ernest Schwiebert.

Patagonia Baker Lodge, Chile

(800) 547-4322

OrvisTravel@Orvis.com

Patagonia Baker Lodge offers anglers the chance to fly fish in Chile while enjoying some great wild country at the same time. The Rio Baker begins its journey to the Pacific Ocean 170 miles south of Balmaceda. From its headwaters in Lake General Carrera, the Baker flows through a spectacular mountainous countryside. It is flanked on the north and south by the Patagonian ice fields, and its banks are richly forested. Many big fish in spectacular settings.

Europe

Salvelinus Lodge, Spain

(800) 547-4322

OrvisTravel@Orvis.com

Lush valleys, high-altitude meadows, and the Pyrenees Mountains are the setting for trout fishing in northern Spain. Ivan Tarin has a quality fly-fishing business that covers more than two dozen valleys across 200 miles of mountain terrain. Catch browns, rainbows, zebra (Mediterranean) trout, and brook trout in streams and lakes that can only be accessed with special permission in the high Pyrenees.

Appendix C:
Further Reading

The following titles are the books I read prior and during the writing of this book. All of them, especially those written long ago, contain often overlooked, basic, and very useful concepts and suggestions.

Behnke, Robert J. *About Trout: The Best of Robert J. Behnke from "Trout Magazine."* Lyons Press, 2007. Behnke's essays answered an abundance of questions I had about trout. Fine reading and an excellent resource.

———. *Trout and Salmon of North America.* Free Press, 2002 This is the definitive book on the subject. That's all there is to it.

Blandford, Percy W. *Knots & Splices.* Arc Books, 1965. My favorite book on knots—simple, direct, good illustrations, and easy to understand.

Brooks, Charles E. *Larger Trout for the Western Fly Fisherman.* Barnes, 1970. A thorough treatment of fishing for big trout out West by a master of the process. Anything Brooks has written, I've read more than once.

———. *Nymph Fishing for Larger Trout.* Crown Books, 1976. I've learned more about catching large browns from this book than any of the hundreds of others I've read/studied. Must reading.

———. *The Trout and the Stream.* Nick Lyons Books, 1974. Further and refined examination of the ideas discussed in his first book.

Camp, Samuel G. *Taking Trout with the Dry Fly.* MacMillan Company, 1930. A wonderfully succinct, knowledgeable book. Camp keeps it simple but insightful.

Francis, Chris J. *Brown Trout Fly Fishing.* Frank Amato Publications, 1977. A nice book of observations on catching brown trout. Some I agree with, some I don't.

Gierach, John. *The View from Rat Lake.* Pruett Publishing, 1989 Finely crafted essays on the nature of fly fishing.

Gingrich, Arnold, ed. *American Trout Fishing.* Alfred A. Knopf, 1966. Contains a previously unpublished essay by Theodore Gordon titled *American Trout Fishing,* along with writings by Charles K. Fox, A. J. McClane, Roderick Haig-Brown, Lee Wulff, and Guy Jenkins, among others.

Gordon, Theodore. *American Trout Fishing*. Alfred A. Knopf, 1972. Gordon's work is filled with truths that pop off the page. The long-ago guys knew their stuff and kept things readable and succinct in the process.

Haig-Brown, Roderick. *A Primer of Fly-Fishing*. Frank Amato Publications, 1964. Solid information from one of fly fishing's master anglers and writers.

Halford, Frederick M. *The Dry-Fly Man's Handbook*. Derrydale Press, 2000. Originally published in 1913, Halford's work, while dated in places, still holds up, especially about drag and conditions.

Harrop, Rene. *Learning from the Water*. Stackpole, 2010. If you want to see and learn how the inveterate tacticians and technicians on the Henry's Fork go about fly fishing, read this book. In my mind, it's already a classic.

Heacox, Cecil E. *The Compleat Brown Trout*. Winchester Press, 1974. This is more than an entry-level book on brown trout. There's good information here.

Hellekson, Terry. *Popular Fly Patterns*. Peregrine Smith, 1977. My favorite book of fly patterns. There are other books with newer, improved, modified, bastardized ties, but this book is the one I turn to.

Heywood, Joseph. *The Snowfly: A Novel*. Lyons Press, 2000. Fiction is good for the angling soul, especially when it involves a quest of mythic proportions that careens from Viet Nam to Michigan's Upper Peninsula (aka God's Country). Heywood's Woods Cop mysteries are good, too.

Hughes, Dave. *Wet Flies*. Stackpole Books, 1995. An excellent companion to Sylvester Nemes's works, with Dave's own takes on the fishing, tying, and theory of wet flies. You can't go wrong with a Dave Hughes book.

Jones, Robert F. *The Run to Gitche Gumme*. Lyons Press, 2001. Bob's last novel and one of his best, with lots of action, mayhem, and fishing for enormous trout in the North Woods.

Krinanec, Karel, and Friends. *Czech Nymph and Other Related Fly Fishing Methods*. 2nd ed. Grayling and Trout Publishing, 2007. These guys are a little crazy, but who isn't? They know how to catch trout with nymphs—and I mean really know. The book also reaffirmed some ideas I had about fishing close to fish with nymphs.

La Branche, G. L. M. *The Dry Fly and Fast Water*. Greycliff Publishing, 1998. Originally published in 1914, La Branche reveals an abundance of information that hasn't been improved on in nearly a century. A classic that earns the distinction.

LaFontaine, Gary. *The Dry Fly: New Angles*. Greycliff Publishing, 1990. Gary was one of the true good people in fly fishing. He was a class person all the way down the line. This book epitomizes his intuitive and penetrating look at fishing.

———. *Trout Flies: Proven Patterns*. Greycliff Publishing, 1993. The title says it all, with patterns ranging from a Stub Wing Bucktail to a Cat's Ear to a Were Wulff. Always prime information in Gary's books.

Marinaro, Vincent. *In the Ring of the Rise*. Crown Publications, 1977. Groundbreaking exploration of trout feeding habits, among many other subjects discussed here, with superb photography.

Martin, Darrell. *Fly-Tying Methods*. Lyons Press, 1987. Martin's book is one of the most straightforward, best-explained books on fly tying I've come across and now own. He knows how to fish, how to design and construct flies that catch fish, and, most importantly, explains how to tie these patterns. A classic. And his book The Fly-Fisher's Craft: The Art and History is a wonderful historical treatise on fly fishing.

McClane, A. J. *McClane's New Standard Fishing Encyclopedia*. Henry Holt, 1974. This book, while dated in places, is the stuff of dreams and knowledge. I've spent many hours wandering through this one looking up everything from the Bimini twist to Sunapee trout to fishing the Rio Rancho in the Yukon.

Nemes, Sylvester. *The Soft-Hackled Fly Addict.* Self-published, 1981. Further explorations of a long-forgotten but highly successful method.

———. *The Soft-Hackled Fly and Tiny Soft Hackles.* 2nd ed. Stackpole Books, 2000. If you want to add a method to your repertoire that will take fish when others won't, read this book.

———. *Two Centuries of Soft-Hackled Flies.* Stackpole Books, 2004. An excellent compilation of writings on the subject ranging from Scotcher in 1800 to Pritt in 1886 to Reid in 1971.

Norris, Thaddeus. *Norris on Trout Fishing: A Lifetime of Angling Insights.* Derrydale Press, 1994. A thoughtful overview on many aspects of fly fishing published long ago, but worth reading now.

Proper, Datus. *What the Trout Said.* Lyons and Burford, 1996. In one concise book, Proper has culled much of the wisdom of the great fly tiers and added his own insights into the feeding behavior of fish. This is one of the finest books ever written on attracting trout with an artificial fly.

Prosek, James. *Trout of the World.* Stewert, Tabori & Chang, 2003. Prosek's art and observations about species of brown trout around the world are superb.

Schwiebert, Ernest. *Matching the Hatch.* MacMillan Company, 1969. In its own way, a groundbreaking book by Schweibert. Some readers consider him to be wordy and a bit of a snob. I don't. He harkens back to an era when fly fishing was not peopled with yahoos who consider what some of us love an industry, a way to make a quick buck. Read all of his books. The time will be well spent.

———. *Nymphs.* Winchester Press, 1973. Another groundbreaking work by Schwiebert on the subject of nymphs that holds its own with newer titles.

Scott, Jock. Greased Line Fishing for Salmon. 5th ed. Seeley Service & Company, 1961. Excellent book on how to fish wet flies written before Nemes published his works.

Skues, G. E. M. *The Essential G. E. M. Skues.* Edited by Kenneth Robson. Lyons Press, 1998. A collection of writings by Skues that runs the gamut of his observations and experiences encompassing well more than a half-century of fly fishing.

————. *Itchen Memories.* Herbert Jenkins, 1951. Published after Skues's death, this is a charming memoir of fishing one of England's most famous chalk streams, filled with wisdom about taking trout.

Reynolds, Barry. *Mastering Pike on a Fly.* Johnson Books, 2004. Pike are like brown trout—freshwater sharks, extreme predators. What works in Reynolds's book leads to taking big browns.

Rosenbauer, Tom. *Reading Trout Streams.* Nick Lyons Books, 1988. Tom is a consummate fly fisher and a fine person. Anything he has to say on the subject is worth serious consideration.

Traver, Robert. *Anatomy of a Fisherman.* Peregrine Smith, 1978. If I could choose only two books on fishing to take with me wherever I roamed, one would be *McClane's New Standard Fishing Encyclopedia.* The other would be this one—witty, funny, insightful, thoughtful. They will never come any better than John Voelker, aka Robert Traver.

Whitlock, Dave. *Imitating and Fishing Natural Fish Foods: Everything an Angler Needs to Know About the Foods That Trout Eat and How to Imitate Them.* Lyons Press, 2002. This book of only 132 pages is a must for any fly fisher. Whitlock's books are all great, but this is my favorite.

Woolner, Frank. *Trout Hunting.* Winchester Press, 1977. The title says it all. Frank knows his stuff.

Lurking just below the surface . . .

Index

About the Author

The author of sixteen published books, including *Flyfishing Adventures: Montana, Yellowstone Drift: Floating the Past in Real Time, Arctic Aurora: Canada's Yukon and Northwest Territories, Coyote Nowhere: In Search of America's Last Frontier, Chasing Fish Tales,* and *Kicking Up Trouble,* John Holt is currently working on a novel based on the murder of his brother on New Year's Eve, 1979. His work has appeared in publications that include *The Fly Fish Journal, Men's Journal, Fly Rod & Reel, Fly Fisherman, Gray's Sporting Journal, Audubon, E—The Environmental Magazine, Briarpatch, Jeep, Big Sky Journal,* and *Outside.*

With his wife, Ginny, he spends much of his time traveling and fishing throughout Montana, Wyoming, the western Dakotas, Alberta, British Columbia, and the Yukon and Northwest Territories. Other activities include collecting vintage bamboo fly rods and reels, and reading murder mysteries by the likes of Charles Willeford, Karen Fossum, Mark Smith, and Arnaldur Indridason. He's lately been listening to music by Radiohead, Coltrane, Imogen Heap, Jeff Beck, and Captain Beefheart, among others. He spends a good deal of time trying to figure out what his black cats, Elmer and Harvey, are trying to show him.